Y0-AAB-031

A Citizen's Guide to THE GRAY REPORT

Prepared by the editors of
The Canadian Forum

new press/Toronto/1971

ISBN 0-88770-122-1

new press
Order Department
553 Richmond St. West
Toronto 133, Ont.

Editorial Offices
84 Sussex Ave.
Toronto 179, Ont.

Manufactured in Canada

Annual subscription ($5.00) are available from the

CANADIAN FORUM LIMITED

56 Esplande Street East,

Toronto 1

CONTENTS

GRAY'S ELEGY

(Reprinted from the December 1971 issue of The Canadian Forum.)

The present issue of the FORUM offers our readers, and the citizens of this country, an abbreviated but authentic version of the Gray Report on foreign ownership. Our purpose is to induce the Government to release the full text and, we hope, to act on its recommendations.

We are conscious of our responsibility in the step we have taken. We ask only that the reader judge this matter on its merits after he has read the text.

The present Report is moderate in tone, and comprehensive in its research and in the scope of its findings. The policy proposals are feasible and straightforward. The report is an excellent document of its kind. It should prove a sound guide to those who are concerned with the level of foreign ownership in this country and to those who are seeking further information.

As the introduction to the Gray Report makes clear, the genesis of this document goes back at least two years to a memorandum submitted to Cabinet by the Minister of Finance in November 1969. Public discussion, of course, antedates this by many years, as far back as Walter Gordon's Royal Commission on Canada's Economic Prospects *in 1957 through to the Watkins Report and the Wahn Report. It is no exaggeration to say that public concern with the whole question of foreign ownership is deep and genuine. The Cabinet obviously had no choice except to deal with this matter, and Herb Gray was brought into the Government in 1969 especially to take on this*

*task. The expectation from the beginning was that the
report would be a public document, but in May 1971,
Prime Minister Trudeau began to hedge on the question of
publication, a turn of events that created some annoyance
in the media. Perhaps the journalists were not alone in their
dismay, for as the authors of the Gray Report themselves
acknowledge in their introduction, "The Canadian public,
including the business community, is expecting a policy
statement from the Government." We agree.*

*The Gray Report appears as the third major govern-
mental study of foreign ownership and the most detailed
in its recommendations. Readers will recall that the
Watkins Report was published in February 1968, and the
Wahn Report in August 1970. Both Reports had as a
central recommendation, the establishment of a special
governmental agency to supervise the operations of foreign-
owned companies in this country. The basis of this recommendation derives from the peculiar flexibility of the
multinational corporation in regard to its global decisions
on location, production, research and development, marketing arrangements, internal pricing procedures, royalty and
dividend payments and numerous other areas. As the Gray
Report so well indicates, we cannot continue to rely on the
bygone doctrines of laissez-faire or the discipline of the
old competitive economy to protect the interests of the
public in the age of the global corporation. Its planning
proceeds out of its head office on a world-wide scale. The
maximization of its own overall profit position bears no
necessary relation to the interests of a particular host
country. What is incumbent on national governments is to
screen closely the extent and implications of these operations in their own domestic environment, to lay down a set
of effective guidelines embodying the national interest,
and to intervene where necessary to apply and enforce
them. This central message of the Gray Report confirms
independently a twice-told tale.*

*The present version of the Gray Report has been edited
down to about one-quarter of its original size. The document
was issued as a Memorandum to the Cabinet entitled
"Domestic Control of the National Economic Environment:*

The Problems of Foreign Ownership and Control" and was dated May 1971. We have tried to retain all the conclusions and policy recommendations which are scattered throughout the Report while omitting repetitious passages and those likely to be of secondary interest to the average citizen. Nothing has been added to the original text, but we have occasionally re-arranged some paragraphs to enhance the clarity of the argument. Although we have not obtained the last two chapters of the original text, we have the strong impression from the complete table of contents that the main reasoning and the major conclusions are present here.

Such a process of pruning and selection necessarily stands in danger of offering a somewhat biased or distorted presentation. We have exercised reasonable care under the pressure of time to do as full justice as we were able to the elaborate argument of the text. Personal judgements, however, stand to differ on the passages of intrinsic interest to the general reader. We hope, as we have stated above, that the full text will be made available by the Government to all who wish to examine the full report.

A political judgement was also required in our decision to take this initiative at the present time. In an interview with Charles Lynch, the Prime Minister expressed, on behalf of many people in this country his concern that the United States would "buy up more and more of our country," if the present policies of the Nixon administration were to continue. It seemed to us however, that the onus of responsibility on the issue of foreign ownership lay primarily with the Canadian rather than with the American Government. Further reports appeared to indicate that the Cabinet had decided, after lengthy consideration, against publication of the report. This prompted us to take this initiative. After these many years, neither the facts surrounding foreign investment in Canada, nor possible policies available to us, can, by any stretch of the imagination, continue to be regarded as a state secret. If our present strained relations with the United States have revealed anything at all, then surely our economic vulnerability and our absence of forethought in this carte blanche process of integration, seem to be the chief lessons of the day.

The Old Guard in the Cabinet, semper fidelis, *continues to press its policies of hopeful sleep-walking into the future. An aroused Canadian public now demands an entirely different answer. We invite you to let us and the Government know where you stand.*

THE EDITORIAL COMMITTEE

1/INTRODUCTION

THE PROBLEM

The high and growing degree of foreign, and particularly U.S., control of Canadian business activity has led to a Canadian industrial structure which largely reflects the growth priorities of foreign corporations. Many of these corporations invested in Canada to extend the market for their manufactures. Subsequently, Canada has become locked into accepting a pattern of innovation and technological development originating abroad. Other corporations invested in Canada to extract resources for home consumption. In either case, to the extent that these corporations were influenced by their home environment, their investment decisions reflected the industrial priorities of foreign governments and economies. This in turn has contributed to the integration of the Canadian economy into the world economy in a way which could make it increasingly difficult for Canada to realize its growth and employment objectives.

It has as well led to the establishment of "truncated" firms for which many important activities are performed abroad by the parent company, with the result that the development of Canadian capacities or activities in these areas is stultified.

These developments have made it more difficult for the Government to control the domestic national economic environment. They have also influenced the development of the social, cultural and political environment in Canada.

The increasing internationalization of some important sectors of industry and the growth of the multinational enterprise (MNE) as an institutional development of foreign direct investment add a further dimension of complexity to the Government's ability to control the national economic environment. Many U.S. companies, for example, started their international operations in Canada but now have branches in many countries. The existence of production facilities in various countries increases the power and flexibility of the MNE in its dealings with the Canadian Government; and intensifies the problems of truncation by reducing the likelihood of the MNE moving more activities to Canada, particularly since other governments actively intervene to control non-resident owned corporations in their jurisdiction. The bargains other governments strike with an MNE may have an adverse impact on Canada, particularly if Canada lacks similar bargaining levers or does not choose to use them.

BACKGROUND

It emerged that there were three broad policy alternatives which the Government might adopt to deal with the problem of foreign ownership and domestic control:

a. the introduction of a screening process, i.e. a government agency with the power to negotiate for better performance from foreign direct investors (e.g. further processing), and with the power to block investment that does not make a net contribution to the Canadian economy or that does not accord with the objectives of the Government;

b. the delineation of further key sectors in which foreign ownership would be regulated;

c. the introduction of across-the-board ownership rules, (e.g. 51 per cent Canadian ownership) and other structural changes relating to the use of Canadian managers and directors.

Particular attention has been given to defining a potential role for a screening process, as during the course of the analysis, it emerged as probably the most effective and least costly way of dealing with the problems.

2

THE DEVELOPMENT
OF
FOREIGN INVESTMENT

THE NATURE AND DETERMINANTS OF FOREIGN DIRECT INVESTMENT

Host (Canadian) Environment

Since Confederation, consecutive governments have emphasized the need for rapid Canadian development. This emphasis on growth led to the emergence of important "gaps" as the demands of the economy normally exceeded the supply of domestic, human and non-human resources: needed technology was not available from Canadian sources; capital to finance a particular venture or category of activity could not be found (or Canadian financial intermediaries were unable or unwilling to fund certain undertakings); entrepreneurial talent to identify and fill a particular need in the Canadian market seems to have been lacking; and Canadians tended to look to foreign sources (the U.S. in particular) for certain goods or services. The existence of these "gaps" makes it considerably easier for foreign investment to penetrate the Canadian market.

It is significant that needed technology was not purchased (e.g. through licences) and needed capital came in the form of direct investment rather than portfolio investment to support the growth of Canadian firms. This suggests that the gaps were more than financial, that they were in fact entrepreneurial or technological in nature. Of course foreign direct investment, because it often provides a missing ingredient, tends to stultify the development of this ingredient (Canadian technology or entrepreneurship) and aggravate the existing gaps.

The reasons for the existence of an entrepreneurial gap is a complex psychological and sociological question. Three potential explanations can be suggested:

a. Canada's colonial status may have led to a mentality of looking abroad for the new and the better in goods and services;

b. The Canadian education system — especially in Quebec — was heavily geared to a classical curriculum and it did not turn out the engineers and business graduates needed to lead the development of an entrepreneurial and innovational society;

c. Financial institutions and to some extent the senior business executive positions generally have reflected a degree of clannishness and a reluctance to deal with those who were not members of the right social circle. This lack of social mobility in Canadian society may also have frustrated the growth of indigenous innovation and entrepreneurship.

It should not be concluded that this analysis suggests that Canada become self-sufficient and do everything for itself. Some of the "gaps" identified may be a reflection of the economic soundness of relying on foreign sources to fill certain needs which are more effectively performed abroad. However, it is clear that some of the gaps identified are the result of deficiencies in Canadian public policy and/or institutions and help explain why the market system has not been able to perform adequately without governmental intervention.

Canadian governments — Federal and Provincial — have deliberately created a framework to attract foreign capital to meet the growth aspirations of the country. This has helped to stimulate the inflow of the various ingredients of growth — large pools of capital, entrepreneurship and risk-taking, technology, management "know-how" and skilled manpower. With a few notable exceptions (e.g. C.N.R., C.B.C., Air Canada), Canadian governments have relied heavily on the private sector, creating an environment attractive to business investment — rather than looking to public ownership as some countries have done to fill needs not met by domestic private interests. Incentives have generally been available on a non-discriminatory basis to Canadian and non-Canadian investors alike.

Spawning Distinctiveness: The Home Economy

The Canadian economy has tended to produce relatively few manufacturers with a distinctive capacity. The U.S. economy, on the other hand, has produced a good many and their products are marketed internationally by trade and direct investment abroad. Factors which tend to generate such products include a high level and rate of growth of per capita income, the size of the market, a highly competitive environment, and the cost of labour.

At the consumer level, high and rapidly growing real incomes, large markets, and a competitive environment create wants for increasingly sophisticated products, encourage innovation and product differentiation, and provide better opportunities for new products to gain acceptance. The size of the market influences the rate of development and adoption of new products since a larger market holds out the prospect of greater profits. Consequently, large, wealthy, growing and competitive markets are more likely to foster innovation. In addition to the factors mentioned above, the development of producers' goods is influenced by factor endowments; the educational system and the abundance of skilled labour; growth aspirations; and the quality of the specialized institutions and services that support entrepreneurs. High wages induce more capital intensive production and more advanced technology.

These underlying determinants have favoured economies like that of the U.S. — and increasingly in Europe and Japan as these economies develop — as sources of distinctiveness. A smaller industrialized nation like Canada tends to find its comparative advantage for international activity in undifferentiated manufactured goods such as steel or aluminum ingot. These tendencies however are not immutable and governments can and do influence or alter these underlying determinants.

The Recipient Economy

The host economy must be basically open or receptive to the products offered by the capital or goods exporting company. For this receptiveness to exist in the case of consumer goods, conditions and characteristics similar to those of the "home" economy must exist, e.g. similar consumer tastes, real income, and spending capacity. Costs of labour, production techniques, factors of production and educational levels influence the receptiveness to or appropriateness of foreign producers' goods and technology. Physical proximity also has a significant influence on the receptiveness of an economy to distinctive foreign products.

Historically, Canada has not sought to keep out foreign products. Very few tariffs have been prohibitive. Canada has provided fertile ground for the sale of products of U.S. origin and U.S. based firms have seen Canada as a logical extension of their market, given the cultural and social similarities, political stability, physical proximity, benefits of advertising spill-over, and the increasing ease of access as communications and transportation improve. This Canadian "openness" has been reduced to a certain extent by import barriers, but these did not preclude the profitable extension of U.S. based firms into Canada by direct investment or trade.

To this list of factors which have facilitated foreign penetration of the Canadian markets should be added the existence of political and economic structures which supported these underlying tendencies. Both trade and direct investment presuppose a degree of institutional cooperation (e.g. banks and capital markets), and governmental support which make it safe for private business transactions to occur.

This analysis is not meant to imply that an economy is exclusively either a creator or recipient of distinctiveness. An economy may develop distinctiveness in one area and purchase it in another. As Europe and Japan continue to develop, a growing degree of interpenetration is taking place between their economies and that of the U.S.

In summary, it can be said that trade and foreign direct investment in manufactures have many common determinants, e.g. similar tastes, comparable stages of industrial development, etc. It is economies that are alike that relate in the field of manufactures. But what makes one country the exporter or investor and the other the importer and recipient is the possession of distinctive capacities. It is large, growing, wealthy and competitive economies that tend to spawn distinctiveness. The exploitation of distinctiveness tends to bring a kind of "monopoly" profit, but this does not mean that the host economy does not benefit.

Foreign Direct Investment: Manufacturing

Foreign direct investment is a complex combination of costs and benefits: easy access to foreign entrepreneurial talent, technology, capital and markets must be offset against truncation; the competitive stimulation in certain cases must be counterbalanced by the restrictions on competition in others; the provision of export markets in certain cases must be counterbalanced by export restrictions in other cases; increased economic growth, jobs, tax revenues, etc. must be offset against the effects of foreign direct investment on our industrial structure; and so on. It is the existence of both costs and benefits that poses the problem for Canada. If there were no benefits it would be a simple matter to block all foreign investment.

The foreign investor often has first call on real Canadian resources with the result that the structure of our economy and the priorities of our industrial development are in a large part determined by corporate decisions taken in a foreign environment and often reflect the economic and industrial priorities of the foreign government or economy.

The transfer of "distinctiveness" (i.e. special technical advantages) by a foreign investor tends to involve a "package". For example, a foreign proprietor of a particularly attractive technology might make access to its use conditional upon the purchasing of components, the payment of a managerial fee for services or all the equity financing for the project. These inputs may be overpriced to the host economy and represent a kind of monopoly gain to the investor if his incremental cost for them is low or zero and his transfer price is set at a fully allocated cost. The tying of inputs in the foreign investment package also increases the barriers to entry for potential Canadian producers. The direct investment package may also attach a number of restrictive conditions which reduce the flexibility and impose added costs on the host economy, e.g. tied procurement, export restrictions, or limitations on research and product development.

Reference has often been made to the greater risk involved in foreign direct investment. This greater risk, together with the desire to maximize the returns by concentrating in the parent company, functions for which there are economies of scale or other savings, leads the foreign controlled firm to reduce the scope of its activities and the amount of investment it commits in the foreign market with the result that operations tend to be "truncated".

Truncation means potentially less decision making and activity in Canada — fewer export opportunities; fewer supporting services; less training of local personnel in various skills; less specialized product development aimed at Canadian needs or tastes; and less spillover economic activity. It ties the subsidiary to the parent in a relationship of dependence, e.g. for technology, components and services. Truncation also increases the flexibility of the parent in repatriating profits, e.g. by allowing it to charge the subsidiary for components or services at a rate which is significantly above the incremental cost of the firm. Truncation is inherent in the nature of foreign direct investment. A foreign manufacturer sets up operations in Canada to extend the market for his distinctiveness. He does not set out to maximize the activities and operations of the subsidiary.

Because of the risk involved and the close connection with market extension, direct investment tends to favour large firms — firms that have the necessary resources, and aim at establishing a global market position based on the market and economic power developed in their home economy. To the extent that foreign investment is pre-emptive, e.g. designed to prevent a potential Canadian competitor from developing, it will further reduce competition in the Canadian economy.

Foreign direct investment acts as a transmission belt for the entry of foreign laws into Canada. It brings cultural influences which may or may not be desirable. Foreign direct investment also creates difficulties for the domestic political process, Canada's image abroad, and the formulation of foreign policy.

Foreign Direct Investment: Natural Resources

The major determinants of foreign direct investment in resource industries are the benefits of backward vertical integration for foreign processors and fabricators. The other major conclusions emerging from this analysis of the nature and determinants of foreign direct investment in the resource industries are not substantially different than in the case of our analysis of manufacturing. Foreign direct investment involves a pool of costs and benefits for the Canadian economy. This pool differs from that in manufacturing on both the cost and benefit side: greater importance of large pools of capital; greater contribution to regional development; greater emphasis on the employment of capital relative to labour; more development of resources as opposed to manufacturing. As in the case of manufacturing, resource development gives the foreign investor a special return. The extraction of resources gives their proprietor a return in excess of the cost of retrieval plus a fair or normal profit.

The benefits of foreign direct investment in resources are generally well understood for they are in many cases implicit in the reasons which gave rise to it. The large pools of capital needed for specific projects have not always been available in Canada. The provision of large and secure markets has eased the problems of financing and facilitated the achievement of scale economies. The provision of technology and managerial skills may have been important in some cases but, in general, has not been nearly as significant or beneficial as in the manufacturing area. This is partly because Canada has developed its own technology in the resource field and partly because it was relatively easy to import foreign technology in the form of machinery. Regional development has been accelerated, especially in remote areas. High exports and the resultant contribution to Canada's balance of payments have allowed Canadians to enjoy a higher standard of living than might otherwise have been possible. However, the net balance of payments effects of any particular project is difficult to determine and may in fact be negative.

But there have been costs as well. Some of them are not as fully understood as the benefits.

Foreign direct investment in the resource industries has led to a relatively greater emphasis on the use of capital over labour. A number of domestic policies (e.g. tax incentives) have contributed to this. While jobs in resource exploitation are generally high paying, there are relatively few of them. (Mineral production in 1970 accounted for about 7 per cent of GNP but only 1.4 per cent of the labour force was employed in mining.)

Foreign direct investment to supply foreign markets with resources tends to have first call on domestic capital and real resources. This could prevent potential Canadian users of these financial and real resources from developing the manufacturing and service industries in Canada.

Canada's openness to direct investment has meant that Canadian industrial development and priorities have in large part been determined by foreign corporate interests and the industrial policies of other governments. This has led to a greater emphasis on the resource sector in comparison with manufacturing. Furthermore, other governments will put increasing emphasis on obtaining secure supplies for their resource needs and will likely continue to find Canada relatively attractive. Under these circumstances, external forces, through direct investment in particular, will continue to shape the industrial activity of Canada. Overdevelopment of the resource sector may not accord with Canadian objectives or priorities including the long-run employment objectives for a growing population.

Depending on their ultimate balance of payments effects and the reactions of Canadian monetary authorities, large capital inflows to develop Canadian resources could exert excessive pressure on the Canadian exchange rate and further aggravate the problem of developing manufacturing activity in Canada. A higher exchange rate increases the price of exports relative to imports and puts pressure on exporting and import-competing industries. Similar pressure developed in Canada after the resource boom in the '50's and the value of the Canadian dollar rose to parity with the U.S. dollar.

Foreign direct investment and vertical integration in the resource area have led to the truncation of activities with further processing and fabricating, in particular, taking place abroad. Truncation also reduces the development of supporting industries. Vertical integration has also made it more difficult for an independent Canadian operation to enter the industry either at the extraction or at the processing level. While resource activity, particularly that which is foreign controlled, involves high levels of exports, most of the transactions are in non-arms length relationships. The net benefits to Canada in tax revenues and foreign exchange earnings may thus be affected.

Resource development places heavy demands on the public purse for infrastructure in remote areas, subsidized transportation facilities and various tax incentives to the investors. Many of the disadvantages outlined here are only partially attributable to foreign investment; others must be rectified by changes in domestic policy.

Natural resources are in demand internationally. Canadian priorities on the other hand may require less emphasis on this sector or the addition of further activities such as processing and fabricating, if Canadian objectives are to be met. Canadian resources still appear attractive to foreign buyers. While the circumstances certainly vary from commodity to commodity, there would appear to be a scope for influencing the distribution of benefits between the foreign investor and the Canadian economy.

Size and Growth of MNE

Some indication of the size and growth of the MNE is given by the following figures. The book value of U.S. foreign direct investment increased from approximately $7.5 billion in 1929 to $70.8 billion in 1969. Sixty-two of the top 100 U.S. corporations have production facilities in at least 6 foreign countries and 71 of the top 126 industrial corporations for which information is available are reported to have one-third of their employment abroad. It is estimated that about 80 per cent of all U.S. foreign direct investment is accounted for by some 200 firms (e.g. General Motors, Chrysler, Ford, Singer, Esso, ITT, etc.). About 100 non-U.S. firms comprise the major MNEs of the rest of the world (e.g. Nestlé, Shell, Lever Brothers, etc.). This means that about 300 MNEs, two-thirds of them U.S. controlled, dominate the field of foreign direct investment. It is estimated that the production activities of U.S. subsidiaries in other countries result in well over $200 billion a year in sales. The subsidiaries which other countries control probably account for about $100 billion of production in the U.S. and $150 billion of production in other countries.

Even on the basis of very conservative estimates, it seems clear that MNEs will continue to grow and become increasingly powerful institutions. It is estimated by one observer that the annual value of output in foreign markets by MNEs will rise from the present level of about $300 billion to over $2,000 billion by 1990 and account for half the "free world" GNP compared to some 15 per cent in 1969. The world's economy will be dominated by 300 or 400 super MNEs. It will not be unusual for an MNE to have 1 million employees. Most of these projections are based on rather simple techniques and are open to serious question. However it is probably true that the total value of production by MNEs will exceed $1,000 billion by 1980.

Assuming the present wave of mergers continues (encouraged by government policy in certain cases, e.g. in Britain and Europe), the size of MNEs will tend to grow rapidly. This same tendency for greater and greater agglomeration will presumably reduce the overall number of corporations involved, simply because the world's total stock of large business firms must be expected to grow less rapidly than the rate at which mergers link them together. Thus we will probably have fewer MNEs but they will be larger.

While European and Japanese MNEs will continue to grow rapidly, it is likely that U.S. rooted MNEs will continue to dominate for the foreseeable future.

While the challenges arising for national governments from the MNE are not qualitatively different from the challenges posed by bilateral direct investment, the characteristics of the MNE noted above (size, financial strength, flexibility, power, and planning ability) mean that the challenges are greater, more complex, and more difficult to deal with. In particular, the power of the MNE to play the government of one country off against the government of another needs to be closely watched. It may well be that cooperation between governments will be needed in the long run if this power is to be contained.

The growth of MNEs is likely to lead to greater integration of national economies. This will tend to reduce the abilities of national governments to control their own economic destiny. The logic of this development is that national governments and MNEs are on a collision course. Because at present most large MNEs are U.S. controlled, ethnocentric in orientation, and rely on their home government for protection, in the short run, this is likely to lead to increasing confrontation with the U.S. For the government of a relatively small country like Canada this could have serious adverse consequences, for Canada could find itself confronted not only by the subsidiary and its parent but also the parent's government. Since other countries are likely to find themselves facing some of the same problems as Canada, it is possible that Canada could ally itself with some of these other countries, (e.g. Japan and some members of the EEC) to further its interests in the face of U.S. controlled MNEs.

A host government is not without some leverage in dealing with the MNE. Location on its territory of some assets of the MNE gives it some bargaining power. Through these assets it can exercise some influence on the parent and, perhaps, the home government, as appears to have happened under the Canada-U.S. Auto Agreement.

In the longer run, the development of MNEs, especially if they begin to lose their ethnocentricity, could lead to growing confrontations with *all* national governments. It should not be forgotten that MNEs are beginning to constitute a growing problem for the U.S. Government's ability to implement its domestic and other policies, e.g., the U.S. balance of payments problem. The U.S. Government is also coming under increasing pressure from U.S. labour to prevent the "export of jobs" said to accompany direct investment by U.S. MNEs. The U.S. concern over the behaviour of U.S. rooted MNEs forecasts a longer run possibility, viz., that the MNE becomes a power in its own right not particularly tied to any one national jurisdiction except perhaps by reason of incorporation.

There is another point worth noting in this connection. If MNEs were to develop to the point where they become the major organizers of production in the world, they would undoubtedly be a major power. But power responsible to whom? At the moment this power is wielded largely by national governments responsible to their electorates. In a world dominated by large and powerful MNEs, to whom would non-elected boards and management of multinational enterprises be responsible?

POSSIBLE COURSES OF ACTION

It seems clear than the rise of the MNE creates a new situation that requires new powers in the hands of governments. It is unlikely that the traditional tools of controlling the business environment — tax, tariff, competition, and monetary policy — will be sufficient.

There appear to be three broad possible courses of action open to national governments in the face of the challenge of the MNE:

   a. to resist the MNE where it adds nothing to national economic objectives;
   b. international cooperative action between governments to control its activities and, failing this;
   c. national measures to ensure that the host economy derives maximum benefits.

Although the data in Table 1 are further evidence of the continued upward trend in foreign ownership, the absolute numbers in some cases must be treated with some caution, due to double counting.

A more representative picture is shown in Table 2, which covers only non-financial firms, even though some technical problems do remain.

In the year 1968, assets of firms which were 50 per cent or more non-resident owned were worth $50.7 billion. Hence the often publicized $50 billion needed for "buying back" Canada. However, this number does not represent the book value of foreign direct investment in Canada. For one thing, as already suggested, it contains some double counting. The assets column in Table 2 excludes a part of this double counting but not all of it. The remaining double counting is estimated to be around 17 per cent. The value of assets of non-financial 1968 firms, after all double counting has been removed, is estimated at $32.7 billion.

Even this figure does not represent the book value of foreign direct investment in Canada. Some non-resident owned firms have minority Canadian shareholders. The assets of others include debts owed to Canadians. In short, any figure which one might select as representing the value of foreign direct investment in Canada would require a precise indication of what was included and excluded by this expression. An estimate somewhat below $30 billion (in 1968) might be a fair indication of the order of magnitude in that year.

But even this does not tell what the cost of "buy back" would be as it reflects book value, not market value. No estimates have been done on the market value of foreign direct investment in Canada. For example, a major consideration influencing the market value is whether the initiative for the purchase of the controlling shares of a firm rests with the buyer or the seller. If all foreign investors in Canada became concerned about the Canadian economic or political environment and decided to get out, the pressure to sell would be such that many would have to settle for much less than book value. On the other hand, if Canadian entrepreneurs were to decide that they wanted to acquire a large number of foreign controlled firms, they might well find themselves obliged to pay substantially more than the book value or even current market values to get controlling interest in some of these firms.

In mining, according to CALURA, almost 63 per cent of assets, 60 per cent of sales, 55 per cent of profits and 48 per cent of taxable income are accounted for by non-resident owned firms. Thus, in terms of assets and sales, non-resident participation is greater in mining than in manufacturing. On the other hand, large parts of the remainder of the economy remain predominantly Canadian owned.

It should be noted, with respect to Table 4, that several of the industries are ones in which there is a large public investment (such as power, gas, water and transportation) or restrictions of foreign investment (financial institutions) or both public investment and restrictions (communications). It should also be noted that the figures in Table 4 probably overstate the degree of non-resident ownership, as a significant amount of the investment capital in some of these industries is in unincorporated businesses which do not report to CALURA.

Table 3, based on the most recent CALURA publication, provides figures on the percentage of non-resident ownership in various industries as measured by assets, sales, profits and taxable income.

Within the manufacturing industries, non-resident ownership is greatest in the petroleum and coal products industry. The others in which there is very great non-resident ownership include: rubber products, transport equipment, tobacco and chemicals. In each of these cases, more than four-fifths of the assets, sales, profits and taxable income are accounted for by non-resident ownership.

Other industries in which non-resident ownership exceeded one-half of industry assets include machinery, electrical products, and primary metals. In contrast, the industries in which Canadian ownership is greatest include: furniture, printing and publishing[1], leather products, wood, food and beverages, and textiles and clothing. Taking manufacturing industries as a whole, non-resident owned firms accounted for a higher proportion of profits and taxable income than for sales; and it would appear that in many individual manufacturing industries, the profitability of non-resident owned firms in relation to sales was greater than for resident owned firms. While the absolute data are not sufficiently accurate to enable us to put forward precise figures on the comparative profitability of Canadian and non-resident owned firms, the higher profitability of non-resident owned firms tends to lend strength to the earlier analysis regarding the ability of the foreign controlled firm to exploit its distinctive advantages in Canada. Finally it is also evident from the data that the high technology industries are generally non-resident dominated.

Regional Distribution of Foreign Controlled Firms

As might be expected, Ontario and Quebec, as the two most important centres of industrial activity, were, for the most part, also the most important centres of foreign ownership. In the case of Ontario this also reflected the fact that foreign ownership in that province was higher than the national rate in the manufacturing and

1. The value and size of the printing industry is greater than the value and size of the publishing industry. This helps explain why the "Printing and Publishing Industry" can be largely Canadian owned, in spite of the high degree of foreign control of Canadian publishing houses.

mining sectors and either close to, or above average in most other sectors. Foreign ownership in Quebec was somewhat below national levels in all sectors and services but utilities. Table 5 shows the relative importance of foreign owned firms to each region by industrial sector using the criterion of taxable income.

Foreign ownership of the manufacturing industries as measured by taxable income averaged 64 per cent over the 4-year period under review. In only one region, British Columbia, did Canadian-owned companies earn a greater proportion of taxable income than foreign-owned ones. Non-resident ownership was highest in Ontario at 70 per cent, followed by the Prairies (61 per cent), Atlantic Provinces (60 per cent) and British Columbia (44 per cent).

The proportion of taxable income contributed by non-resident-owned corporations in the mining industries reached 55 per cent on average during the 1965-1968 period. Regionally, 89 per cent was attributable to foreign-owned companies in the Atlantic provinces, 76 per cent in the Prairies, 59 per cent in Ontario, 51 per cent in Quebec and only 27 per cent in British Columbia.

Table 6 shows the regional distribution of foreign-owned firms by industrial sector, again using the criterion of taxable income.

Ontario was the most important centre of foreign-owned manufacturing activity. Some 58 per cent of the taxable income accruing to foreign-owned corporations in this industry was earned in Ontario. This was about two and a half times the proportion earned in Quebec, the next most important province in this respect, and reflected the pre-eminence of Ontario as Canada's principal centre of manufacturing and the fact that a larger proportion of Ontario's taxable income originated with foreign-owned corporations.

Most foreign-owned taxable income from mining was derived from the Prairies, Quebec, and Ontario, which accounted for 38 per cent, 25 per cent and 21 per cent of the Canadian total compared with 8 per cent for the other two regions[2].

How the Growth of Foreign Control is Financed

Foreign controlled firms are financed by:
a. the internal cash flow of foreign controlled firms in Canada;
b. raising of equity or debt in the Canadian capital market;
c. new direct investment from abroad;
d. portfolio investment from abroad.

2. It seems likely that the figures for British Columbia are now much higher than they were in the period 1965-68. Japanese investment has increased since then. Also, the fact that the criterion is taxable income may give a downward bias, since some of Japanese controlled mines may not have been paying taxes towards the end of the 1960's.

The DBS has constructed a new series of data to show how foreign-controlled firms financed their business between the end of 1946 and the end of 1967. Over these years, the Bureau estimates that the book value of foreign controlled investment increased by $24.5 billion. Of this amount, it is estimated that each of the sources supplied the amounts shown in Table 7.

By adding in capital consumption allowances and depletion, a complete picture of the sources of finance is obtained (Table 8).

Of the $43.8 billion in financing available over the entire period, $9.7 billion was derived from foreign sources — a little more than 22 per cent. In the period 1960-67, only 19 per cent was obtained from abroad, with a corresponding proportionate increased use of Canadian sources, including proportionately greater use of retained earnings, capital cost allowances and Canadian capital markets.

According to the Department of Industry, Trade and Commerce survey, based on 326 reporting firms which accounted for more than 900 subsidiaries, the net external funds (i.e. external to the company) obtained from foreign sources between 1965 and 1969 decreased sharply as a proportion of net external funds obtained from all sources. However, this was due more to a reduction in funds obtained from foreign markets than to increased demands on the Canadian capital markets.

The implication of the above Tables is clear. Firstly, they show the obvious — that if new direct investment were to be entirely excluded from Canada, foreign control would continue to grow in absolute terms, due both to internal generation of finances by the firm and by their ability to raise external funds in the Canadian capital markets. Secondly, over 60 per cent of the financing for the expansion of foreign control in the 1961-67 period came from Canadian sources, (i.e. excluding capital cost allowance) so that if the Government wishes to control the rate of growth in foreign control effectively, it would not be sufficient to look exclusively at new direct investment. It would also be obliged to take account of the finances obtained from Canadian capital markets and the application by the individual firms of the internal cash-flow While there are also some objections to such measures, particularly in respect of internal cash-flow, some such intervention would be necessary to control the expansion of the foreign controlled sector. The desirability of such measures is considered later in the Memorandum.

Conclusions

All the data confirm that foreign control now constitutes a very high proportion of Canadian corporate activity and that it is particularly concentrated in resource exploitation and manufacturing. Within manufacturing, foreign control is concentrated in particular industries, including most of the science-based industries, such as transport equipment, chemicals, machinery and electrical products. In 1968, according to CALURA, close to 40 per cent of the assets of non-financial firms were non-resident controlled.

As for regional distribution, it is apparent that Ontario has received a larger proportion of foreign investment in relation to the size of its economy than other parts of the country, while other parts have obtained correspondingly less.

The most recent Investment Position data show continued growth in foreign control and the CALURA data on ownership reveal the same trend. Based on both sources, we can say that while the rate of increase of foreign control is not as great as it was in the 1950's, the trend still appears to be upward. Moreover, statistics cited on the proportionate growth in savings of foreign controlled firms suggest the possibility of further increases in 1968 and 1969 in the Investment Position data.

FOREIGN TAKEOVERS

Implications of Takeovers

Notwithstanding the lack of full information, some generalizations can be made about foreign takeovers Firstly, foreign takeovers often do not result in any significant growth in Canadian employment. Nor do they necessarily release funds to be used elsewhere in the Canadian economy for creating jobs. For example, payment received by the seller is often wholly or partly through share swaps which effectively mean that the foreigner takes control of a Canadian enterprise with the Canadian acquiring a share in the foreigner's Canadian subsidiary; or the funds used by the acquiring firm may actually be borrowed in Canada, also implying that no net new funds are being released.

Even if the non-resident brings his capital with him and pays the seller in cash, and the seller subsequently invests the capital in job creating activity, this may add nothing if the Canadian Government has had to borrow money on the Canadian capital market to buy the foreign currency of the non-resident to keep down the exchange rate. In that kind of case, the same impact could be had if there had been no takeover, and if the Canadian seller had borrowed directly the money which was used to start the new job creating activity.

Another possibility is that a Canadian seller may receive only a small initial payment with additional payments to come from future earnings. The Canadian, even if paid in cash, might invest abroad or use all or part of it for consumption. In all of these possibilities, no new jobs are being directly created. Indeed, even if he deposits the money in an institution which eventually invests it in job creating activity, the time lag can be considerable. This, of course, is not to say that in all circumstances funds released in a takeover may not be used for creating jobs elsewhere — only that the chances are significantly slimmer than is the case when a new firm is started. This latter point is most important, of course, when a large Canadian firm in a particular industry is acquired. In that instance, new job creation, at least at first, is not very likely.

Firms which prefer to take over a Canadian controlled firm rather than to start from scratch are more likely to be ones which have less to offer to the Canadian economy. Indeed, as indicated previously, the foreigner may be buying the Canadian firm to obtain its technology, markets or management. By the same token, in purchasing a large or leading Canadian concern, the foreigner is less likely to be adding as much new competitive thrust as he would be if he were to start up a new firm or to take over a small one.

In all the above comments, the emphasis is on likelihoods, not absolutes. Indeed, as was also implied above, foreign takeover obviously can involve the saving of jobs in firms which would otherwise be shut down. It can introduce new competitive stimulus, new technology, additional management capacity and fresh markets. In some circumstances, it may also release funds for job creation elsewhere in the economy. Furthermore, although a takeover normally involves concentration of production as opposed to new competition, this may be more appropriate in some industrial situations.

Thus, it is concluded that takeovers are less likely to provide economic benefits than are new investments. Where the takeover does not provide a significant contribution to the economy, or where it involves some net cost to the economy, it seems appropriate to question the desirability of allowing it to be implemented.

One complication, of course, is that there may be conflict between the private and public interests. In cases of takeovers involving no significant benefits, the Canadian owners may wish to sell for perfectly legitimate reasons and not unnaturally want the best price. At the same time, it should be observed that the Government already does intervene substantially in the economy in this way by prohibiting foreign takeovers in all the sectors referred to generally as key sectors (e.g., banks, federally incorporated financial institutions, broadcasting, etc.) and in blocking certain domestic mergers. Furthermore, most of the arguments against takeovers set out in the previous two paragraphs apply with greatest force to the taking over of firms with very substantial assets, i.e ., firms which are least likely to be personal or family firms and most likely to be trading publicly.

Conclusions

The data on the number and value of takeovers and on the reasons for them are not as comprehensive as they might be, although they are probably as good as can be found in any other country. Because of the great importance of foreign takeovers in Canada, a more systematic gathering of such data should be an essential part of a better information programme.

Notwithstanding shortcomings in the data, it is evident that takeovers have been a major route through which foreign control has grown. Furthermore, it is believed that the economic benefits of such takovers are normally far fewer than those obtained through the starting up of new firms, particularly when the takeover involves large Canadian controlled firms. For this reason, it is believed that public policy can reasonably contain a degree of bias against foreign takeovers, especially of large Canadian firms, and that it should be up to the purchaser to demonstrate the value of his purchase to the economy.

TABLE 1
FIRMS 50% OR MORE NON-RESIDENT OWNED
TOTAL ALL INDUSTRIES 1965-8

Year	Assets $Million	%	Equity $Million	%	Sales $Million	%	Profits $Million	%	Taxable Income $Million	%
1965	35,560	24.5	18,780	34.9	30,078	33.4	2,671	40.1	1,764	44.4
1966	40,468	25.8	20,324	35.3	33,967	33.6	2,907	40.0	1,699	42.2
1967	44,825	26.0	22,328	35.7	36,730	33.5	2,913	39.3	1,652	40.4
1968	50,766	26.8	25,008	37.0	41,301	34.7	3,514	41.3	2,070	42.2

TABLE 2
NON-FINANCIAL FIRMS 50% OR MORE NON-RESIDENT OWNED
TOTAL ALL INDUSTRIES 1965-8

Year	Assets $Million	%	Equity $Million	%	Sales $Million	%	Profits $Million	%	Taxable Income $Million	%
1965	27,973	36.0	15,076	40.0	29,478	34.6	2,522	46.0	1,694	48.6
1966	31,794	37.4	16,414	40.7	33,307	35.1	2,660	44.1	1,624	46.4
1967	35,244	38.00	17,973	41.5	35,958	35.0	2,618	43.8	1,561	44.6
1968	39,442	39.4	19,839	43.0	40,380	36.3	3,182	47.1	1,969	46.9

TABLE 3

Manufacturing Industry	Percentage of Non-Resident Ownership as Measured by			
	Assets	Sales	Profits	Taxable Income
Food and beverages	31.3	27.1	29.4	30.9
Tobacco	84.5	80.1 82	82.7	83.1
Rubber products	93.1	91.5	90.1	88.4
Leather products	22.0	21.4	25.2	27.3
Textiles and clothing	39.2	28.5	54.9	54.6
Wood	30.8	22.2	23.8	23.0
Furniture	18.8	15.5	20.4	23.2
Printing, publishing and allied	21.0	13.2	22.0	22.7
Paper and allied	38.9	40.7	39.8	39.0
Primary metals	55.2	51.1	62.4	64.4
Metal fabricating	46.7	45.0	64.7	62.6
Machinery	72.2	72.7	78.1	87.2
Transport equipment	87.0	90.6	89.8	88.7
Electrical products	64.0	62.7	78.0	88.1
Non-metallic mineral products	51.6	42.3	47.2	52.9
Petroleum and coal products	99.7	99.6	99.7	99.4
Chemicals and chemical products	81.3	81.1	88.9	89.1
Miscellaneous manufacturing	53.9	51.2	72.1	72.6
Total – All Manufacturing	58.1	55.0	63.4	62.4

TABLE 4

Industry	Assets	Degree of Non-Resident Ownership as Measured by Sales	Profits	Taxable Income
Construction	13.8	10.8	12.6	16.8
Transportation	8.4	9.3	17.9	14.9
Communications	0.4	0.3	0.6	2.9
Public Utilities	15.7	25.3	20.8	28.3
Wholesale trade	31.4	28.8	30.5	30.6
Retail trade	21.2	19.9	31.4	32.7
Financial industries	12.6	11.5	18.9	14.2

TABLE 5

PERCENTAGE OF CORPORATIONS TAXABLE INCOME EARNED IN EACH INDUSTRIAL SECTOR AND REGION ATTRIBUTABLE TO NON-RESIDENT-OWNED COMPANIES, 1965-1968 AVERAGE

Industrial Sectors	Maritimes	Quebec	Ontario	Prairies	B.C.	Canada
Agriculture, forestry, fishing and trapping	42.9	–	14.3	6.2	25.2	20.7
Mining	88.8	40.6	59.3	76.5	26.7	55.0
Manufacturing	59.6	60.3	70.0	60.5	44.1	63.8
Construction	9.7	12.1	19.0	23.0	42.6	20.6
Transportation, storage, communications and public utilities	16.2	44.0	20.9	19.3	12.0	22.1
Wholesale trade	17.6	32.2	39.7	38.5	30.8	35.7
Retail trade	30.4	27.2	36.3	52.2	40.5	37.4
Finance	21.8	22.3	25.6	28.3	26.7	30.6
Services	24.4	41.9	39.1	40.6	27.8	38.7

TABLE 6

PERCENTAGE OF TAXABLE INCOME OF FOREIGN-OWNED CORPORATIONS ATTRIBUTABLE TO EACH GEOGRAPHICAL REGION BY INDUSTRIAL SECTORS, 1965-68 AVERAGE

Industrial Sectors	Maritimes	Quebec	Ontario	Prairies	B.C.	Canada
Agriculture, forestry, fishing and trapping	6.5		13.0	4.3	76.2	100.0
Mining	8.0	24.9	21.2	38.1	7.8	100.0
Manufacturing	2.7	23.7	58.2	8.7	6.7	100.0
Construction	3.6	12.1	35.7	22.1	26.5	100.0
Transportation, storage, communications and public utilities	8.3	29.9	23.4	30.1	8.3	100.0
Wholesale trade	2.6	22.5	48.6	17.0	9.3	100.0
Retail trade	6.9	15.8	37.5	25.5	14.3	100.0
Finance	4.3	23.3	45.4	17.7	9.3	100.0
Services	1.9	30.5	39.3	15.3	13.0	100.0

TABLE 7
SOURCES OF EXPANSION FUNDS FOR FOREIGN CONTROLLED ENTERPRISES

	1946-60		1960-67		1946-67	
	$ Millions	%	$ Millions	%	$ Millions	%
Capital Inflows from Countries of Principal Owners	5,316	39.2	3,631	33.1	8,947	36.5
Portfolio Investment from Abroad	399	2.9	373	3.4	772	3.1
Sub-total	5,715	42.2	4,004	36.5	9,719	39.6
Retained Earnings	4,164	30.7	4,124	37.6	8,288	33.8
Canadian Capital	2,631	19.4	2,334	21.3	4,965	20.3
	12,510	92.3	10,462	95.5	22,972	93.7
Other Factors	1,045	7.7	496	4.5	1,541	6.3
	13,555	100%	10,958	100%	24,513	100%

TABLE 8

	1946-60		1960-67		1946-67	
	$ Millions	%	$ Millions	%	$ Millions	%
Total from Above	13,555	59.6	10,958	51.7	24,513	55.8
Capital Consumption Allowance	8,241	36.3	9,323	44.0	17,564	40.0
Depletion	929	4.1	903	4.3	1,832	4.2
Grand Total	22,725	100%	21,184	100%	43,909	100%

3

MAJOR DETERMINANTS OF CANADA'S DEPENDENCE ON FOREIGN DIRECT INVESTMENT

CANADA'S BALANCE OF PAYMENTS, SAVINGS AND CAPITAL MARKETS

The sections which follow discuss some of the central concerns of this Memorandum: the need for direct investment in relation to Canada's balance of payments requirements; the adequacy of domestic savings in relation to Canadian capital investment requirements; and the performance of Canadian capital markets in helping to satisfy Canadian capital investment needs.

Balance of Payments

The first point examined is whether direct foreign investment is needed for reasons related to the balance of payments. The analysis shows that the current account has been gradually improving over the past decade.

In view of the strength of the current account, it is concluded that there is no immediate need for direct foreign investment for balance of payment reasons. Indeed, the present balance of payments situation presents the Government with an opportunity to intervene in the area of direct investment, to achieve some of the objectives outlined in this Memorandum, while at the same time providing some additional modest resistance to further upward pressure on the exchange rate.

Furthermore, the analysis suggests that even when Canada is experiencing a modest current account deficit, means are normally available for dealing with the deficit without relying on direct investment from abroad, for instance, by importing debt capital or by some restriction of capital outflows. It is thus further concluded that, from the perspective of the need to finance a current account deficit, there will be no particular requirement for inward direct investment, at least for the next 3 or 4 years. With the need to resist the continued upward pressure on the exchange rate at this time, there is good reason to hold down additional foreign capital investment in Canada.

This does not mean that all foreign investment ought to be rejected over the next several years for it can and sometimes does bring non-financial economic benefits, for instance, new technology and export markets not otherwise available. It is being suggested, however, that since the exchange rate situation and the level of unemployment are such that only limited amounts of foreign capital can be absorbed, it makes sense to be selective in determining what foreign capital will be allowed to enter. That is, it makes sense to consider the economic consequences of absorbing capital of would-be foreign investors to ensure that only those which would have an overall beneficial effect on the economy are allowed entry.

Indeed, the present circumstances are very propitious for the introduction of some selective screening of direct investment.

Savings

There may be insufficient savings generated in the economy to finance the required level of capital investment, assuming an economy which moves over the next few years substantially closer to a full employment path. This in turn is divided into two separate issues. The first is whether in aggregate terms it is anticipated that sufficient savings will be generated to finance the necessary level of capital expenditures. The second is whether the savings generated domestically are allocated in a way which will ensure that essential capital investment requirements are satisfied; for although domestically generated savings might be sufficient in aggregate, some investment needs might not be satisfied simply because no individual Canadians and no financial intermediaries were making available the necessary capital.

The analysis below does not assume any significant changes in the investment-consumption ratio over the next few years, nor does it depend upon any sweeping changes in tax levels or in Government expenditure patterns. On those assumptions, the question being posed is whether, in aggregate terms, the kind of capital investment programme needed to help move the economy close to a full employment path can be financed from anticipated savings of Canadian

In fact, this question is really identical to the one already raised with respect to the likely future strength of the current account of the balance of payments. A current account deficit implies that

Canadians are currently drawing upon the real resources of the rest of the world and financing them by going into debt or by accepting in perpetuity a foreign claim (i.e., a foreign equity investment) on the economy. By stating that even with a more fully employed economy, Canada will not have a current account deficit in the next 3 or 4 years which will be so big that it cannot be financed by capital imports in forms other than direct investment, it is being said that Canada's anticipated savings rate will be entirely or almost entirely adequate to meet Canadian capital needs.

All of the above factors relate to aggregate considerations and to the macro-economy. They do not necessarily mean that all capital investment requirements which can be financed domestically will in fact be financed domestically.

Over the past 20 years, the proportion of Canadian savings accounted for by non-residents has dropped sharply and in 1970 (and the early months of 1971), Canada was a net saver for the rest of the world.

SAVINGS OF FOREIGN CONTROLLED CANADIAN FIRMS

The above does not take account of the savings of foreign-controlled firms in Canada. An indication of their importance has been provided by the DBS, which has endeavoured to estimate their importance in the 1967-9 period. This unofficial and unpublished calculation showed that in those 3 years, $8.8 billion of $52.8 billion of the gross savings of that period were generated by foreign controlled firms. Of that amount, $3 billion was accounted for by retained earnings, $5 billion in capital consumption allowances and $0.8 billion in depletion. This means that gross savings by foreign controlled firms were equal to 16.7 per cent of the gross savings available to the economy in that period, 34.6 per cent of the gross savings of the corporate sector, 14.2 per cent of the net savings available to the economy and 28.5 per cent of the net savings of the corporate sector. Moreover (as indicated earlier) the savings accounted for by the foreign controlled sector for 1968 and 1969 represented a significant increase over previous years.

Thus, while Canada has recently become much less dependent on foreign savings, a large part of domestic savings are generated by foreign controlled firms.

LIKELY TRENDS

It was pointed out that the non-resident contribution to the economy has been falling for a number of years. In 1970, Canadians acted as savers for the rest of the world. However, this does not mean that it can be assumed that in the future, Canada will not again have a net need for non-resident savings — that Canada will not again require net capital imports to finance a current account deficit.

For one thing, the economy has been operating well below capacity in the last few years. Accordingly, demand for imported merchandise and services has been less vigorous than it would have been in a period of greater economy activity. Furthermore, even in periods when the non-resident contribution to savings is small, it may provide the necessary additional amount of capital expenditure needed to bring unemployment down to tolerable levels. What can be said with confidence, however, is that as the economy moves back to its full employment path, no net non-resident contribution will be needed in the next three or four years which would be so great that it could not be filled through means other than direct foreign investment. Indeed, the only detailed and careful quantitative projections available suggest that these expectations about domestically generated savings are, if anything, unduly conservative.

There are two major qualifications which must be added to the above points. The conclusions above relate to Canada's capacity to save in aggregate the sums needed for adequate investment. They say nothing about Canada's ability to generate some of the other inputs which often accompany foreign capital, such as technology, management skills and export outlets.

Secondly, they do not imply that Canada will not continue to rely heavily on foreign capital markets. Rather, they simply say that, in an aggregate sense, domestic savings should be sufficient or nearly sufficient to meet capital investment requirements at or near full employment. In practice, since there is a relatively free flow of capital into and out of the country, large amounts of Canadian savings are invested abroad and substantial proportions of foreign savings are invested here. This is a point which is dealt with more fully in the next section.

The above does not mean that the savings of Canadians (as in every other country) will be sufficient to meet the requests for them by all prospective users. Demand for housing, social capital, plant machinery and equipment and resource development in the 1970's will be very great. In other words, savings appear to be adequate to finance all or a very high proportion of an economy operating near full capacity, however this should not be confused with the expectation that Canada will have sufficient savings to satisfy all would-be borrowers of capital. The process of resource allocation will remain every bit as difficult as in the past.

Capital Markets

Another determinant of Canada's effective ability to finance domestic economic development is the efficiency of the Canadian capital market and its willingness and capacity to undertake risks and to support entrepreneurship. The analysis here is concerned with the extent to which Canada relies upon Canadian financial institutions to help finance new and generally more risky economic activity and the extent to which foreign sources finance these ventures. If Canada relies heavily on foreign sources, this would clearly reduce domestic capacity to control the economic environment. It would also likely reduce possibilities of increased Canadian ownership.

The evidence available suggests that Canadians finance a much smaller proportion of the growth in productive capacity in Canada than the volume of Canadian savings would permit. This reflects many factors.

Firstly, many foreign controlled enterprises are already in Canada and able to finance expansion out of internally generated funds.

Secondly, new firms enter Canada for reasons exogenous to Canadian capacities in financing, technology or management. For instance, the foreigner may find it profitable to exploit his product or technology in Canada or to obtain Canadian natural resources for supply assuredness and no barriers exist to his doing so.

Thirdly, foreigners take on projects which are judged to be too risky by Canadians. The foreigner's perception of the risk in many cases, however, is different than the Canadian's. The real risk is simply much smaller for him for one reason or another — because an export market is assured, a tax advantage is available, the investment constitutes a smaller part of his investment portfolio, he has greater experience in the business, his cost of money is cheaper or whatever. These are all reasons which help to explain the reason why Canadian savings are not channelled into indigenous development to as great an extent as is possible.

In this context, it should be explained that one assumption underlying this section is that the general shortage of entrepreneurship in Canada can be partly overcome by entrepreneurial leadership by the financial institutions — that all the entrepreneurship need not come from the industrial leaders alone.

Accordingly, this discussion focuses on the risk taking and entrepreneurial activities of Canadian financial institutions and on related factors including the liquidity and capitalization of the capital markets and the degree of competition in the industry. The view taken here is that there are weaknesses and gaps in respect of risk taking and entrepreneurship; the section endeavours to illustrate this, to explain why and to recommend possible courses of action to deal with the gaps.

The gaps are, broadly speaking, to be found in three places; venture capital for new and small firms; expansion capital for small and medium sized firms; and large pools of capital for major resource exploitation projects. There also appear to be inadequacies in the support which Canadian financial institutions provide to regions of slow economic growth. Other gaps, for instance, in respect of the capital needs for housing and for farming are obviously outside the terms of reference of this Memorandum.

As a secondary point, the section is also concerned that lenders generally tend to give preference to foreign controlled firms; and while this preference can undoubtedly be explained by the generally greater size and credit-worthiness of foreign controlled firms as opposed to those that are Canadian controlled, this remains a matter for concern in the context of assisting Canadian ownership.

In playing a comparatively small role in risk taking and entrepreneurship, Canadian financial institutions seem to be reflecting several influences. One is that the historical availability of direct foreign investment has not been conducive to creating within Canada the kinds of institutions and persons able and willing to take on this role. The Canadian capital markets are normally called upon to play a major role in launching major resource exploitation projects; and though they may ultimately supply much of the debt capital to the foreign firms, they do not have a well developed capacity to play more than a limited financial role.

Furthermore, legislative and other constraints upon the investment choice open to the institutions tend to limit their capacity for filling some of the gaps. While intermediation does involve turning low risk short-term deposits into somewhat higher risk long-term investment, the institutions cannot be insensitive to the nature and longevity of the savings it accumulated. For instance, if the institutions are able only to attract demand money, their investment choices are limited. Some amendments to current legislation or practice might ease these restrictions though wholesale change in this area has to be limited by the need for safeguarding the investments of private individuals and by the legitimate competing demands for capital, e.g. for housing or junior government financing.

Conclusion

The implications of these views are clear. The absence of a well developed capacity in the financial industry to assist certain kinds of economic activity in Canada increases the likelihood of such activities being financed from abroad. The shortage of entrepreneurship in the financial industry frustrates the kind of industrial intermediation in Canada which could permit a larger proportion of major projects to be controlled in Canada. The fact that normal risk aversion creates a lender's preference for the generally large foreign controlled firms (though not because they are foreign) reinforces these difficulties.

It is not reasonable to expect that Canada will be able to finance as high a proportion of very expensive major resource development projects (which can run to hundreds of millions and billions of dollars) as of the many smaller industrial kind (where needs can be as low as a few hundred thousand dollars). Surely it is reasonable for some Canadian financing to be done in New York. But the present heavy dependence on foreign financial institutions is greater than it need be for a country with a savings rate and industrial maturity of Canada's and this tends to draw direct foreign investment into Canada in situations where the economics of the project often do not require it, thus exacerbating the problem of domestic control.

One related consideration reflects the concern of the United States authorities about Canadian dependence on U.S. capital markets at a time when the Canadian balance of payments is strong and the U.S. position relatively weak. If the U.S. continues to run a large deficit, the United States Government could, at some future time, decide to enforce substantial restrictions on Canada's access to the U.S. capital markets. In that event, Canada would be obliged to fall back much more heavily on its own capital markets.

THE IMPACT OF CAPITAL MARKETS ON DOMESTIC CONTROL OF CANADIAN BUSINESS

The Financing of Foreign Controlled Business and its Impact on Canadian Controlled Firms

In general, statistical evidence available does not show any great differences between the pattern of financing of Canadian and foreign controlled firms. For example there are no marked differences in ratio of current to non-current liabilities or in debt-equity ratios.

But some differences do exist. For instance, foreign controlled firms appear to place a proportionately greater reliance on short term credit from parent firms than do Canadian controlled firms; and long term advances from individual shareholders and affiliates, as might be expected, are much more significant as a percentage of non-current liabilities for foreign controlled firms than for Canadian controlled. Thus the financing needs of foreign-controlled firms are eased by the fact that they have much larger foreign parents.

This does not mean that foreign controlled firms do not raise money in the Canadian capital markets. To the contrary, they have been making use of Canadian bank loans and the Canadian bond and stock markets.

The Department of Industry, Trade & Commerce survey of 325 subsidiaries shows that between 1965 and 1969 the contribution of Canadian sources (such as banks, bond markets, etc.) to the annual growth in external (i.e. external to the firm) finances of subsidiaries rose from 28 to 73 per cent, with a corresponding drop from foreign sources. By 1969, Canada was financing 35 per cent of the liabilities of these subsidiaries, whereas Canadian sources had been providing only 28 per cent in 1964. While firm proof is not available, it seems likely that a part of the reduced use which U.S. subsidiaries have made of their U.S. sources is a reflection of attitudes created by the U.S. Balance of Payments programme, even though technically it has not been directed against Canada.

Complete figures are not available about foreign controlled firms' use of Canadian capital markets. However, some indication is provided in the following information. Of the roughly $9.6 billion in bank loans to businesses outstanding at the end of 1969, at least $1.2 billion (12 1/2 per cent) were provided to foreign subsidiaries covered in the Industry, Trade and Commerce survey. And since the sample of subsidiaries is not complete, the actual figure must have been a few points higher.

The Bank of Canada has provided data showing what proportion of net new issues of corporate Canadian dollar bonds and stocks were for corporations which were wholly or partly non-resident owned. They show that around 16 per cent of net new Canadian corporate bond issues and 23 per cent new issues of corporate stock were for firms 50 per cent or non-resident owned in the period from 1960 to 1970.

Particularly in periods of tight money, it may be somewhat tougher for Canadian controlled firms to raise money than it would be if foreign controlled firms were not using the Canadian capital markets. While impossible to quantify, this has apparently been of sufficient concern that, in the past, the Governor of the Bank of Canada has requested the chartered banks to pay particular attention to loan applications from firms not having alternative sources of credit and give priority to credit-worthy demands of Canadian customers rather than to subsidiaries which could use the Canadian market to borrow on behalf of their parent firm, especially at times when Canadian rates fall below U.S. rates.

One question which arises from the data is whether foreign controlled firms should have continued access to Canadian capital markets. This answer must take into account the problems for Canadian controlled firms which arise during periods of tight money; the fact that Canadian balance of payments considerations may at times make it preferable for foreigners to borrow in Canada (as at present); and that foreign controlled firms do employ Canadian workers. In other words, their needs cannot be dismissed lightly.

Proposals

To meet the concerns about the capital markets, certain categories of proposals are made below. The reasons for these proposals reflect in part the obvious desire to see more domestic financing and control as an end in itself and related to this, the desirability of reducing the cost of financing new issues. A further very important consideration relates to the proposal for a screening process. To the extent that such a screening process is concerned with improving the returns which Canadians receive from foreign investment, it must have the capacity to bargain from a position of strength. This in turn means that it ought to have available to it an alternative indigenous capacity to do some of the things which the foreigners are willing to do. In the absence of a vigorous merchant banking or venture capital industry in Canada, and a generally greater degree of entre-preneurship in the financial community, the capacity to bargain effectively is reduced.

The paragraphs which follow set out the kinds of proposals which might be helpful when trying to ensure that a greater proportion of the high risk and entrepreneurial financial activity can be done in Canada. While the proposals imply that the Government would be playing a somewhat greater role in influencing the allocation of capital in Canada than it now is, this is an area in which the Government is, of course, already filling a major role — through tax policy, various methods of deficit financing, through transfer payments to provinces and individuals, its pattern of expenditure, the creation of specific public financial institutions to meet deficiency observed in the past in the capital markets (CMHC, IDB, and the CDC), through various federal and provincial grant and loan programs (PAIT, IRDIA, Regional Incentives Act, Small Business Loans Act, Farm Credit Improvement Act) and so forth.

LIQUIDITY, CAPITALIZATION AND COMPETITION

Any measures which can be taken to improve the liquidity of the stock market and the capitalization of the more entrepreneurial parts of the financial industry should have a beneficial spill-over impact on the financing of new issues. Scope for a federal initiative is now limited by provincial jurisdiction in this area. This would include such issues as better disclosure of corporate situations and a national securities commission with power to improve the quality of regulation.

A further possibility is to allow or even encourage new entry of foreign financial institutions into Canada. They tend to have more capital, and thus could improve liquidity and competition. The main concern that one would have about this is that they would distort the allocation of savings, possibly encouraging Canadians to invest abroad or giving foreigners first crack at investing in attractive Canadian ventures. But, if foreign financial institutions were screened prior to entry, a screening agency would require as one condition of the foreigners doing business here that their allocation of funds be made to conform with the kind of framework established by the screening agency. This would increase foreign control of financial institutions but could simultaneously reduce the proportion of foreign control in the non-financial industries.

Incentives are required to get the existing institutions to be more entrepreneurial; secondly, new institutions and/or pools of capital are needed (including possibly foreign firms); finally, there seems also to be a greater role for government. All these factors should improve competition and the benefits which come from it. These are considered further below.

REGIONAL NEEDS

The general lack of entrepreneurial thrust in the financial industry seems to be a particular problem in the regions of slower economic growth.

One way of dealing with this might be through the creation of regional financial institutions; for instance, a regionally based bank. Although real administrative problems undoubtedly exist, one possibility might be a bank free to raise deposits anywhere in the country but required by statute to invest a proportion of its assets in a designated region (e.g. the Maritimes or Quebec). Depositors would presumably be reassured by existing deposit insurance.

Such a bank would only be able to accept deposits and to grow to the extent that it was able to invest profitably in the designated region. The logic of this would thus seem to require that it help to create attractive investment opportunities for itself in that region — that it play the role of entrepreneur. This is one proposal which it is suggested should receive further immediate consideration by the Departments responsible.

OTHER MEASURES

Three other categories of action seem to be in order. One is to try to create incentives and inducements to get the existing institutions to take greater account of their relatively small role in financing new capital stock. Another is to encourage, both directly and indirectly, the creation of new institutions specifically aimed at filling the gaps (in addition to the regional need). Finally, new Government sources of capital could be used.

POSSIBLE INCENTIVES AND INDUCEMENTS

Looking firstly at the kinds of inducements and incentives which can be used to make capital allocation more responsive to the concerns expressed here, several possibilities merit attention. Government measures which would generally increase the liquidity of loans and other debt instruments (such as mortgages) is one possibility. For instance, CMHC already guarantees NHA mortgages, thus increasing the liquidity of such mortgages and creating an incentive for lenders to make more mortgage money available. Similarly, it may be possible for another Government institution (perhaps the IDB) to rediscount certain categories of loans, particularly venture capital for new small business and expansion financing for small and medium-size Canadian business enterprise. A ceiling of possibly $1 million would be put on loans in this category. One principle involved in such a programme should be that the Government guarantee extend only to 80 or 85 per cent of the loan, so that the institutions will have a financial stake in ensuring that the deal is worth backing.

Another possibility is to provide tax advantages to institutions in return for certain kinds of activity. If, for example, it is desirable for financial intermediaries to lend money to small growing businesses needing expansion financing which are not ready for public distribution of their securities, the institutions might be permitted to deduct from income an amount for "bad debt reserves" which need not be substantiated by actual bad debt experience of the tax paying institutions. This technique does not permanently deprive the Government of revenues but defers their collection. So long as the intermediary keeps its total level of loans in the qualified category at the level of the previous year (or increases its level) no tax is paid on the reserve amount (or additional tax deferred dollars are designated in that category). If at a point in time fewer loans are granted, the Government would recapture the taxes.

Yet another possibility is creating incentives for pension funds and life insurance companies to back the kinds of activity being referred to here. Pension funds, for example seem to attach great importance to being able to invest abroad to get anticipated higher returns on their investments. Through the use of tax legislation, it might be possible to allow them to put a certain proportion of their assets in foreign investments in return for putting a fixed proportion in investments in the category of concern here. Under the White Paper on Tax Reform proposals, it is proposed that no more than 10 per cent of a pension funds' assets be invested abroad if the fund is to retain its tax exemption. This could be modified to require that they put more than 10 per cent of their funds abroad in return for investing in certain categories of investment. Inasmuch as pension funds assets are likely to grow very substantially in the 1970's, a measure along these lines might be highly beneficial. Once again a separate technical study would be needed before adopting such a measure.

Under present law life insurance companies may be discouraged from investing in equity capital because of certain provisions in federal law (e.g. regulations covering the valuation of their liabilities) which make it possible for a firm to be technically insolvent in a stock market downturn. Another technical difficulty for companies is how to reflect capital gains in the book value of their assets. These questions should be re-examined to see whether greater investment scope could not be given to these firms without in any way endangering the position of policyholders.

NEW INSTITUTIONS

The above proposals relate to the creation of incentives to encourage the existing institutions to behave somewhat differently. In addition, it is apparent that certain kinds of institutions are lacking on the Canadian scene and consideration should be given to correcting this situation. In particular, there seems to be an insufficient amount of merchant banking in Canada. While the CDC may go some way toward filling this gap, it is believed that substantially more activity is needed here so that the matching up of buyer and seller and of entrepreneur, inventor and financier are all encouraged. The possibility of creating some form of tax incentive to encourage such activity in Canada could also be investigated.

One of the deficiencies which has been noted is the absence of large pools of capital. One way of helping to overcome this, in addition to encouraging the merchant banker, might be through grouping of "the individual" pension funds and life insurance companies. It is possible that the large sums of money they dispose of could be used to fill at least a portion of the capital needs for resource exploitation. Admittedly, the individual pension fund might be running an undue risk in placing a significant proportion of its assets into a manufacturing venture or new resource exploitation. But consortia of these institutions jointly investing 5 or 10 per cent of their assets in higher risk new economic activity should be feasible. as the large sums would allow sufficient diversity to spread the risks and finance much of what is now being financed from the United States. What would be too risky for one institution could be good business and highly profitable for a group acting in concert.

DIRECT GOVERNMENT ROLE

Any of the possible measures outlined above might help to create a better environment for more entrepreneurship and risk taking in the capital markets. At the same time, it is recognized that it may take some time to fill the gaps and it is thus believed that consideration should be given to direct Government intervention. At one end of the spectrum, the CDC should help to fill the gap. But for venture capital and expansion financing, gaps will remain. One possibility here could involve a substantial expansion of Government guaranteed loan programmes through a revamped IDB, which was more concerned with industry and growth than with loans for small businesses of all kinds. For instance. the IDB and GAAP could be combined into a genuine industrial development agency catering to Canadian controlled firms. Both programmes at present are already largely being used by indigenous Canadian enterprises.

ACCESS OF FOREIGN CONTROLLED FIRM TO CANADIAN CAPITAL MARKETS

There remain the considerations set out earlier with respect to foreign controlled firms' access to Canadian capital markets. While balance of payments considerations may create a bias in favour of or against allowing foreign controlled firms access to the Canadian capital markets at any point in time, there remains a general concern about the access of Canadian controlled firms to the Canadian capital markets. Indeed, to the extent that other measures may be successful in encouraging greater financial entrepreneurship in Canada, it is important to ensure that such improved performance did not redound to the benefit of foreign controlled firms only. While funds loaned to foreign controlled firms do re-circulate and may again become available, the net impact of lending to foreign controlled firms is likely to be one of some displacement of Canadian controlled users.

This constitutes one argument in favour of requiring that foreign controlled firms obtain Government approval for all substantial net new Canadian denominated stock or bond issues and substantial net increases in bank credits or loans. The considerations which would determine whether approval would be given would include balance of payments factors, the adequacy of funds available for Canadian users, the economic merits of the investment for which funds were being solicited and the need for foreign participation to make the project viable. Alternatively, new stock and bond issues alone could be subject to Government clearance; this would raise fewer problems with the business community though clearly there would remain much opposition. The latter alternative would also be less effective for the purpose intended.

The above policy proposal is premised on the view that foreign controlled firms are by and large able to raise money from their parents abroad and that they would not be seriously damaged by some screening of their access to Canadian capital. It also reflects a concern about the access of Canadian controlled firms to expansion capital. At the same time, however, it could serve as a vehicle through which, if the Government wished, it could screen the expansion of the foreign controlled sector when this expansion was based on the use of Canadian capital.

GENERAL CONCLUSIONS

To summarize, there are no strong reasons, relating to the Canadian balance of payments or to the volume of domestically generated savings, which would require Canada to rely upon foreign direct investment to maintain a satisfactory rate of economic growth. The main worry is that Canadian savings are not being transmitted by the financial intermediaries to business enterprises for the starting up and expansion of capital stock to the extent that the level of savings in the economy would permit.

As the adequacy of domestic savings has improved, the volume of savings directed by the intermediaries for investment in manufacturing and resources has increased. However, this seems less related to improved entrepreneurship of the financial institutions than to the greater amount of savings being generated domestically.

THE TECHNOLOGICAL IMPACT OF FOREIGN DIRECT INVESTMENT

A number of important conclusions emerge from these facts. Firstly, as a country likely to remain an important importer of technology, it is sensible to take special care in developing a strong capability in buying technology. It has been pointed out that, in the case of proprietary technology, the interests of the proprietor need not coincide with Canada's. Other countries have demonstrated that it is feasible for a Government to intervene in the process of technological transfer to satisfy its own ends. This involves a process of bargaining, both on the terms in respect of which direct investment enters Canada and on the terms of arms length licence agreements.

Secondly, several cogent reasons exist for further strengthening indigenous technological capacity: to reduce the proportion of output which is in truncated forms, to strengthen Canada's bargaining capacity in respect of imported technology, to help create the technological and entrepreneurial environment needed in Canada, and to help create the capacity to buy foreign technology. In this regard, Government support for research and development should continue to be based upon "benefit to Canada" provisions. The danger of Canadian developments being exploited commercially elsewhere or being wasted (by decisions of parent firms to cut back on Canadian R & D programmes partly funded by Government money) reflects the fact that many Canadian subsidiaries are truncated.

Finally, domestic policies ought to reflect Canada's present position as a heavy net importer of potential technology. Current levels of patent protection run counter to the objective of ensuring rapid dissemination of technical information through the economy.

Screening Process

The analysis provides a further argument for the proposed screening agency. The role a screening authority could play in respect of technological transfer is elaborated on below.

In negotiating with would-be investors, and in particular the multinational enterprise, a screening agency, where appropriate, would bargain for the location of research, development and innovative activities in Canada. This is not to say that the screening authority would always be successful in such efforts, but that if it does not do so, it seems likely that progressively less and less of the research activities of such firms will be located in Canada

Secondly, the screening authority would have the capacity to bargain for the importation of foreign technology through arms length licencing agreements, or joint ventures rather than direct investment, when this seemed to be the cheapest or most efficient way for Canada to obtain foreign technology.

Thirdly, for both the parent-subsidiary and arms length relationships, the screening authority could be given the power to look at the terms of royalty agreements, management fees, R & D charges, etc. to determine whether or not they were fair and reasonable.

Fourthly, to the extent that a foreigner may wish or be requested to find a Canadian licencee, he has the power to play one Canadian off against the other and against the alternative, which is to make a direct investment. If the potential Canadian licencee represents access to only 10 per cent of the Canadian market, his bargaining power with the foreign proprietor of technology is not as great as if he can command 100 per cent of that market. At the extreme, the logic of this would suggest that the Government of Canada purchase the technology at the best terms it can achieve and then in turn, either sell, or make freely available, the technology to Canadian industry. Short of such an approach, the screening authority would have the staff to assist a would-be Canadian buyer in searching out alternative sources of particular kinds of technology, to assess the value of the technology and to suggest to the would-be buyer and seller what terms would be considered to be reasonable; that is, the screening authority could act as a counterweight to the bargaining position of the proprietor of the technology.

Domestic Policies

Appropriate changes in the Canadian patent policy should be implemented to ensure that a more rapid rate of dissemination of the knowledge purchased through imported technology is made available to as many Canadians as would wish to use it. This could be achieved through both shortening substantially the period of protection afforded the owners of technology and through arrangements for compulsory licencing by the Canadian licencee.

Indeed, the Government might wish to go further and actively promote the distribution of information on technology to the Canadian industrial community with a view to making Canadian business more conscious of recent scientific and technical developments and alternative sources of obtaining these developments. The screening agency, or another body of Government, ought to be gathering systematically the most up-to-date information on foreign and Canadian technology, whether it is proprietary or in the public domain. Such a service for domestic industry could provide important benefits to the economy, whether or not a screening agency is established.

Canada's Dependence on External Technology

The discussion below considers the extent to which the Canadian economy depends upon outside sources of technology. Several different yardsticks are used to measure the dependence and while no single one is perfect, they all show much the same pattern.

The first measurement is based on patent statistics. While all forms of technology are not patented, patent statistics are often used as a proxy for technological output. Some 95 per cent of patents issued in Canada are registered to foreign owners, of which two-thirds are owned by United States residents. This is one indicator of Canada's dependence on external technology. Another study shows that in a list of 25 countries, Canada is first in percentage of patents which are foreign owned and last in the percentage of patents owned by nationals of the issuing country.

The above suggests that Canada's technological output, compared to other industrialized countries, has been very low. On the other hand, this fact does not in *itself* constitute an argument that Canada should devote more effort to improving Canada's technological output. Before reaching such a conclusion, it would be necessary to conclude that Canada could obtain its inputs more cheaply by developing them at home than by buying them; or that indigenous development would provide greater benefits for the Canadian industrial structure.

In general, multinational firms prefer to concentrate their research activity in their home base. Thus, Canadian subsidiaries in technologically intensive industries are generally not given the opportunity to do proportionately nearly as much research as their parent. Moreover. some of the R & D undertaken in Canada undoubtedly reflects efforts to modify technology to specific Canadian needs. And some of it reflects situations where there are significant cost advantages in undertaking R & D in Canada (including the cost advantage of tax incentives and public funds) which is not offset by an disadvantage of decentralizing of research and development efforts. However, even when a portion of the research of a multinational firm is located in Canada. it is coordinated with the research of the entire international organization, directed from the home base, and thus not necessarily fitted into the productivity activity of the Canadian subsidiary.

THE IMPACT OF DIRECT FOREIGN INVESTMENT ON CANADIAN MANAGEMENT DECISIONS

In general, there are two routes through which foreign firms influence decisions of subsidiaries. One is through centralizing certain decisions in the parent firm and through the establishment of control systems which limit the discretion of the subsidiary (even on issues where it has ostensible autonomy). The other is through the control of appointments to the board of directors and senior executive positions.

These realities reflect the logic of direct foreign investment and the multinational enterprise and the way it is organized. A firm extends its activities abroad as a part of an overall goal and strategy. It may be doing this to obtain new markets or to protect old ones. It may wish to acquire a safe supply of natural resources or to preclude a competitor from getting them. Whatever the motive, the multinational firm is a total business system and inherent in it is some degree of truncation of foreign affiliates. The relationship is not normally a static one under which the parent firm dictates unilaterally the scope of operations of each subsidiary. The management of the subsidiary obviously seeks to influence senior management at headquarters. There is a two-way flow of ideas, arguments and people. But ultimately, the sub-unit — the subsidiary — must accommodate the international strategy of the parent. Almost by definition, this means that it cannot continuously maximize its objectives.

This, of course, implies that the Canadian environment will likely have smaller impact on business decision making of subsidiaries than it will for the Canadian controlled firm. Federal and Provincial Government Ministers and officials are unable to have the close and continuing contacts with the top management of the foreign controlled subsidiary that they have with senior officers of firms like Bell and CPR. It is thus much more difficult to convince the foreign controlled firms to recognize Canadian objectives and needs when they set their priorities. These firms necessarily are involved in the formulation of a global strategy. Moreover, with the continuing revolution in the means of communication, the likelihood is that the headquarters of the international firm will come to exercise a progressively greater degree of control over the decision making of the subsidiary firm.

These factors have adverse implications for the capacity of Canada to generate senior management with the vision and the ability needed to innovate successfully. With the role of the entrepreneur reduced by extensive foreign control, the environment becomes less likely to generate the kinds of persons able to be entrepreneurs; and of those who demonstrate this capacity, it is not unlikely that a significant portion will be drawn to the U.S. The Canadian environment becomes less exciting and less well able to support entrepreneurial abilities.

Thus the kind of environment can develop in which an absence of entrepreneurial management will tend to perpetuate itself, even if Canada has a sufficient number of technical people to carry out important second and third level jobs in finance, production and marketing. Those who set the goals and determine the strategy are in the U.S. At the extreme, this manifests itself in the miniature branch plant replica of the parent, producing the same products at higher costs for a protected Canadian market. Managing a subsidiary of this sort is doubtless demanding from the viewpoint of ensuring efficiency of use of resources. However, it does little to stimulate an entrepreneurial environment or to draw out the entrepreneurial capacities of Canadian management. The kind of rationalization found in the automobile industry has the same impact. Whatever the benefits of the automotive arrangements, it seems most unlikely to generate entrepreneurship or the services which normally surround an entrepreneurial industry. In brief, the direct investment package embodies entrepreneurial capacities when it enters Canada, and thus reduces scope for Canadian entrepreneurial initiative.

It is natural that an economy with the characteristics of the U.S. economy should be more conducive to entrepreneurship than Canada's. With its larger market higher incomes, higher labour costs, more competitive environment, better technological capacity and other factors, it provides great incentives to innovation. Some gap between the U.S. and Canada is not surprising. The danger is that the current U.S. advantage may be so great as to destroy all Canadian capacities for innovation.

Conclusions

While it is not clear if there has been a shortage in the number of Canadian managers available, information on the educational achievement and other related factors about Canadian management suggests that, in comparison to the United States, there has been a management gap.

One effect of a very high degree of foreign direct investment in Canada is that strategic decisions affecting a very large proportion of Canadian business activity are either taken by senior business executives resident outside of Canada or within a central framework established by those resident outside of Canada. This is required by the logic of the multinational firm. This has certain short-run advantages. It may, in some instances, enable a comparatively higher level of technical proficiency to be brought to bear upon particular decisions than is available in Canada. Moreover, it can help provide the entrepreneurial thrust which is often lacking in Canada.

The dilemma is that, in the medium and longer term, the economic and non-economic costs can be greater than the benefits. One of the economic costs is that direct investment is likely to result in truncation of Canadian corporate decision making, leading to sub-optimal decisions for the subsidiary. The impact of these sub-optimal decisions is likely to be felt throughout the Canadian environment. It also is likely to perpetuate the management gap which now exists and to ensure the continued weakness in the entrepreneurial environment in Canada. As for the non-economic costs, these are reflected in the political and cultural consequences of decisions being taken by non-Canadians and by the fact that foreign controlled firms are less likely to be responsive to Canadian priorities.

These considerations in turn suggest two further conclusions and imply a role for a screening authority. Firstly, to the extent possible, every effort should be made to minimize the degree of truncation of foreign controlled firms already operating in Canada. This means that efforts should be made to minimize the constraints imposed upon Canadian subsidiaries, recognizing that there are obvious limitations on what can be done because of the logic of the way in which multinational firms operate. Secondly, this provides a further argument for careful cost benefit analysis of all would-be foreign investment in Canada and reason to question the desirability of investments which bring few benefits. That is, it is being stated that the terms on which foreign investment enters Canada should minimize damage to Canada's indigenous entrepreneurial capabilities.

Finally, as it is sometimes possible to purchase management from abroad (e.g. consulting services, management firms) a shortage of technical skills need not necessarily result in direct investment as a means of obtaining those skills. The use of management on contract in certain Canadian mines is one illustration of this phenomenon. A screening process could help identify situations in which these kinds of alternatives were preferable to direct investment.

4

THE IMPACT OF FOREIGN CONTROL AND INVESTMENT

THE EFFECTS OF FOREIGN CONTROL ON THE EXPORT PERFORMANCE OF SUBSIDIARIES IN CANADA

In trying to assess the effects of foreign control on the export performance of subsidiaries in Canada it is important to bear in mind that some subsidiaries, particularly in the resource industries, have been set up in Canada in order to develop and export resource-based products; other subsidiaries, almost exclusively in manufacturing, have been set up primarily to sell in the domestic market; still others may have been set up because of special advantages in Canada and may serve domestic and some export markets as well. Markets served by a subsidiary are in most cases allocated to it by its parent company as part of its global marketing strategy.

The statistical data thus appear to suggest that the general economic environment is a more important determinant of export performance than ownership. The general business environment is, however, heavily influenced by the high degree of foreign control in the economy. In addition to the existence of restrictions on exports, foreign control may contribute to widening the very gaps which it entered to fill — gaps in entrepreneurship, capital markets and technological development. Foreign control has probably made more difficult the task of developing distinctive capacities based on indigenous development which underlies good export performance. The general business environment cannot therefore be regarded as a complete and independent explanation of the export performance of foreign controlled firms and of the Canadian economy.

This is an important issue since trade in manufactures is increasing more rapidly than trade in resources and the terms of trade are progressively turning against resources. If Canada does not develop greater distinctive capacities as a basis for greater exports of manufactures, the country's share of world trade will progres-

vely decline and increase the problem of maintaining high living
:andards.

Without denying the benefits of affiliation, and the importance
f improving the general business environment in Canada, it is clear
aat there is potential for better performance from some foreign
ontrolled companies. It is known that export restrictions exist
a significant number of cases as part of the marketing strategy of
arent companies or as a result of the extraterritorial application of
reign laws, policies or regulations. Thus, subsidiaries may be
revented from exploiting potential increases in competitiveness
ained through affiliation. While the impact of these restrictions
impossible to quantify, it is likely that they have in a significant
umber of cases reduced Canadian competitiveness: by limiting the
chievement of economies of scale; the scope for managerial
ecision making; the possibilities for R&D and product innovation;
nd tax revenues.

In addition to the existence of export restrictions in some cases,
ere are other reasons for concern:

a. The proportion of inter-affiliate trade is large and increasing.
   In general this trade is not as subject to market forces as arms
   length transactions. The question arises whether these trade
   patterns, based largely on administrative decisions by foreign
   parent companies pursuing their own corporate interests,
   will respond to Canadian policy objectives. For example: a
   high proportion of exports of foreign controlled companies
   is concentrated in the U.S. market. This makes more
   difficult a policy of diversification advocated in the Government's foreign policy review;

b. Other governments appear to be exerting increasing pressures
   on foreign investors to locate export facilities in their
   territory. Experience suggests that foreign controlled companies respond to pressures of this sort (e.g. the Auto Pact,
   Chrysler and Ford in Britain, Otis Elevator in France). Unless
   the Canadian government arms itself with a sufficient number
   of levers and mobilizes its bargaining power, it may find
   foreign investors, particularly MNE's, making deals with other
   governments at Canada's expense.

reening Process

The most promising policy alternative is the use of a screening
ocedure and the mobilization of Canadian bargaining power to
tain more export activity in Canada. Since a substantial degree of

market allocation occurs between parent and subsidiary companies, and particularly within the multinational enterprise, a screening process would seek to increase the allocation of markets to Canada. The existence of a foreign parent and perhaps subsidiaries in other countries would be turned to the extent possible to Canada's advantage, i.e. the international structure of foreign investment would be used as a vehicle for enlarging markets and increasing exports in cases where this is economic. This is in effect what took place under the Canada-U.S. Automotive Agreement.

General Policies Affecting Canadian Export Performance

The success of the screening procedure depends upon Canada's bargaining power. To supplement this approach, the government should foster the development of strong Canadian controlled export-oriented multinational companies in those sectors of industry where the MNE form of organization provides distinct advantages and foreign investment adds no significant benefit. Initially, this policy would probably be most effective in the resource-based industries. In the manufacturing industries the Canadian MNE would probably pose many of the same problems as the foreign MNE in terms of maintaining strategic activities in Canada. Canadian ownership of MNEs would not relieve the government of the need to watch their behaviour carefully.

Other aspects of policy considered elsewhere in this Memorandum will also affect export performance, for example:

a. improvements in the general business environment, e.g. functioning of Canadian capital markets;

b. further processing of Canadian raw materials before exporting;

c. more assiduous administration of the transfer pricing provision of the Income Tax Act;

d. measures to counteract the extraterritorial impact of foreign laws, policy, and regulations;

e. improving the quality of information on the performance of foreign controlled companies.

The implementation of a screening mechanism together with policy changes suggested above should allow Canada to maximize the net benefits it derives from foreign investment in the export field.

THE IMPACT OF FOREIGN CONTROL ON THE PROCUREMENT POLICIES AND IMPORT PRACTICES OF SUBSIDIARIES IN CANADA

The major factual conclusions that emerge from an examination of the impact of foreign control on the procurement policies and import practices of subsidiaries in Canada are:

a. Foreign controlled companies are importing a large and growing proportion of their purchases of goods and services;

b. Foreign controlled companies tend to source their imports in the country of the parent companies. Because of the high degree of U.S. control of Canadian industry, this in fact means purchasing in the U.S;

c. Not only do foreign controlled companies tend to import from the country of their parent companies, they are sourcing a large and growing proportion of their imports from parents and affiliated companies. In 1969, approximately 30 per cent of total Canadian imports were in the form of intra-corporate transactions;

d. Imports tend to be concentrated in manufacturing sectors where there is a high degree of U.S. direct investment and where the U.S. appears to have a continuing dynamic advantage based on high levels of expenditure for research and product development;

e. Foreign controlled companies are more import oriented than Canadian controlled companies, and imports as a proportion of sales are greater for U.S. subsidiaries in Canada than U.S. subsidiaries in other countries.

While this large volume of imports and purchases from parents and affiliates may make good business sense from the point of view of the particular company, and can be most advantageous for the economy as a whole (if the benefits are passed on to the market-place), it can also have a number of serious adverse implications for Canada.

A high level of procurement abroad can retard the development of the manufacturing and service sectors in Canada.

The large and growing volume of Canadian imports accounted for by intra-corporate transactions introduces an increasing degree of rigidity into the structure of trade and the balance of payments making them less responsive to general government policies. e.g. a policy of diversifying sources of imports.

The relatively high proportion of imports in sectors of

relatively high technology where the U.S. appears to enjoy a continuing advantage based on high levels of expenditure on research and product innovation suggests that parent companies will have a bias for expanding in their home market and it further suggests that Canada will tend to be perpetually "behind" unless the Government intervenes to reverse the situation in some sectors of particular importance to Canada.

The existence of a high degree of vertical integration in the procurement process involving a Canadian subsidiary and its foreign parent constitutes a significant barrier to entry which makes it difficult for an independent Canadian supplier to enter the market for the particular component or end product.

Large volumes of inter-affiliate trade increase the scope for transfer price activities detrimental to the Canadian treasury.

There thus appears to be some reason and scope for trying to get greater procurement activity in Canada. To this end, at least three alternative policy approaches are open to the Government. These are:

    a. the introduction of mandatory rules on Canadian participation;

    b. mandatory procurement in Canada of a certain proportion of purchases; and

    c. the use of a screening process.

Mandatory Canadian Participation: Ownership Rules

There is no assurance that mandatory Canadian participation (e.g. requiring a foreign controlled firm to sell 51 per cent of its voting shares to Canadians) would lead to greater procurement in Canada. While in general, Canadian controlled firms are less import oriented than their foreign controlled counterparts, Canadian participation is unlikely to increase procurement in Canada substantially because the links that lead to greater imports by foreign controlled firms would continue to exist. Canadian participation could however have some impact on the level of transfer prices.

Mandatory Canadian participation would also introduce an added degree of protectionism into the Canadian economy by making it more difficult and costly for a foreigner to establish in Canada. This could be counterbalanced in certain instances by reducing trade barriers.

Procurement Rules

Another alternative — one which would ensure high levels of procurement in Canada — would be the introduction of an arbitrary procurement rule, e.g. all foreign controlled companies must make 90 per cent of their purchases in Canada. Leaving aside for the moment the discriminatory character of this approach, the high degree of protectionism involved could be quite costly. This approach also ignores that there are real economies in vertical integration which government policy should seek to ensure are passed on to the Canadian economy. However, the possibility of such rules, relating to individual sectors and emerging over time from experience in the particular sector, should not be excluded.

Selective Approach: A Screening Process

A screening process could be the least protectionist and hence the least costly of the possible policy alternatives because of its flexibility. It could in fact contribute to the efficiency of the Canadian economy. It could seek to reverse procurement decisions that were based on arbitrary and non-economic factors which contribute neither to the welfare of the particular Canadian firm nor to the country as a whole. In those cases where procurement from the parent is in the best interests of the firm but not necessarily in the best interests of the long-term economic development of Canada, a screening process could bargain for the location of the next expansion in Canada in cases where this is economic. The new production facilities in Canada could serve, for example, the Canadian and European markets with the MNE acting as a channel for Canadian exports to European subsidiaries. The extent to which the screening process can secure this type of investment for Canada will depend upon many factors including the costs of production, access to foreign markets, transportation costs, etc.

In those cases where the parent is purchasing at arms length and it does not make economic sense for the Canadian subsidiary to produce the product or component itself, the screening process could seek to ensure that Canadian suppliers have an opportunity to bid for the supply contract.

THE IMPACT OF FOREIGN DIRECT INVESTMENT
ON DOMESTIC COMPETITION

Manufacturing

The evidence indicates the large size of foreign owned firms, their dominant position in many Canadian industries, and the fact that the industries which they dominate tend to be concentrated and often characterized by product differentiation. Foreign investment may simply introduce concentration or product differentiation into Canada with little or no offsetting benefit.

This can be particularly restrictive of Canadian competition where foreign entry is achieved through the takeover of a Canadian firm — or where the dominance of a foreign firm already in Canada is increased by such an acquisition (e.g. the Shell purchase of Canadian Oil; the Gulf purchase of B.A. Oil; the Merck, Sharpe and Dohne purchase of Chas. Frosst, etc.).

Similarly, the spreading of fixed costs over larger markets by foreign owned firms or MNE's can benefit Canada. The economies of large scale might permit Canada to acquire various valuable inputs at a lower cost than indigenous production would involve. The same result would flow from Canadian firms operating in a sufficiently large market.

However, there are a few industries in which the Canadian market is too small to operate a firm of a minimum size to realize the economies of scale. The Canadian environment is not, however, likely to be able to produce these efficiencies in many industries if it attempts to support a large number of plants and firms, each producing a full range of products. Foreign investment behind tariff protection creates this kind of structure in many manufacturing industries.

Even where there are economies in the integration of Canadian production with a foreign firm, the question remains whether the benefits of the economies are transmitted to the Canadian market. If a foreign firm (or Canadian firm) is under no pressure to do so, the savings would be taken in the form of increased profitability for the parent in one form or another. Where the competition for firms in Canada is import competition, Canadian prices will tend to a level of U.S. prices, plus transportation, plus tariff costs (assuming a U.S. producer is the one having easiest access to the Canadian market). Savings from foreign investment which do not get passed on to the Canadian market place are of no benefit to Canada.

The advantage of the foreign firm, particularly U.S. based consumer product firms, may lie in its capacity to meet U.S. marketing patterns in Canada — i.e. to produce a wide variety of styles or models of a given product using the parent's product designs; to make frequent (generally annual) design changes; and to support a substantial advertising campaign at prices which an independent Canadian firm could not match. In this way, the advantages of spreading fixed costs is taken in the form of cost increasing, product differentiating techniques rather than in price reducing cost savings. This constitutes an advantage for the Canadian consumer only if he is genuinely benefitted by the U.S. market demand patterns.

Even if the foreign owned subsidiary pays a pro rated price for these inputs of product design and promotion, the large scale facilities and international operations of the parent firm reduce the cost below that which would have to be borne by an independent firm attempting to match product proliferation, frequency of change, or distribution and marketing techniques. These techniques are, however, forms of intercorporate rivalry that constitute "product differentiation" rather than price competition. Where this pattern of demand and promotion becomes firmly entrenched, entry opportunities for a Canadian owned firm are significantly reduced.

The foreign firm might enjoy a degree of product differentiation which is based on advertising spill-over from the U.S. or other source, or upon market power which is rooted in the effective domination of the distribution of a product or domestic activity. This form of advantage for the foreign firm similarly offers no real benefits to Canada and reduces the competitive forces in the Canadian industry involved.

Aside from the potential advantages enjoyed by a foreign firm, parental backing might provide easier access to capital from internal resources of the firm or from the financial markets in Canada or abroad. The boost which this offers a foreign firm — based largely on size, which, as noted earlier, is generally fairly typical of foreign firms and MNE's — also makes it more difficult for an independent Canadian firm to enter or compete effectively. Where this easier access to capital is not based on efficiency or economies of scale — or is based on efficiencies which are not passed on to the Canadian market — Canadian industrial efficiency is adversely affected by foreign ownership.

While this analysis has primarily considered the potentially adverse aspects for competition which flow from foreign investment, the competitive advantages of the foreign owned firm can also work to Canada's advantage. In some industries, Canadian firms are likely to find entry difficult. In fact, entry without the advantages of having a foreign parent may be virtually impossible. These advantages include the capacity to enter in a truncated form — capitalizing on the economies of scale which come from the centralized performance of many of the functions at the parental head office or elsewhere in the corporate structure. Under these circumstances, new foreign investment can stimulate domestic competition, induce innovation and cost saving by all the Canadian firms, and benefit the Canadian economy.

Natural Resources

If economically attractive resources are owned by foreign processing firms needing the inputs for their own operations, independent operation of processing facilities is made more difficult.

Canadian activities in the natural resource sector are characterized by significant degrees of vertical integration — as is this sector of most economies in the world. The high degree of foreign ownership in this sector has been noted. The primary motivation for this integration and foreign control is the desire of the foreign firms to maintain their strength in their home markets — rather than to increase their domination of the Canadian market. It has, nevertheless, resulted in barriers to entry and concentration in the Canadian resource industries.

The average firm in the mineral industry is over two times larger than the average manufacturing firm (assets of $4.2 million versus $1.9 million). It is more capital intensive than its manufacturing counterpart, e.g. in 1967 $1 in sales required assets of $1.96 in the mineral industry and $0.90 in the total manufacturing industry.

The average size of mineral industry firms controlled by non-residents is over six times larger by all standards of measurement than that of firms controlled by Canadians. Average assets for foreign controlled firms were $26 million in 1967 versus $3.6 million for Canadian controlled firms. Whereas foreign controlled firms represent 11.4 per cent of total firms, they own 71 per cent of industry assets. These generalizations also apply to the various sub-sectors of the mineral industry, e.g. assets per foreign controlled firm in the mining industry are about four times the assets of Canadian controlled counterparts.

The big foreign controlled firms are particularly concentrated in petroleum and coal products (24 firms with average assets of $198 million), primary smelting and refining (28 firms with average assets of $134 million), primary metals (60 firms with average assets of $52 million), and metal mining (63 firms with average assets of $32 million). The 8 largest firms in petroleum accounted for over 80 per cent of industry sales in 1968. The four largest firms in primary smelting and refining account for nearly 90 per cent of production.

Conclusions

Domestic policy on competition can resolve some of the concerns raised here. Since mergers are part of the concern of the Combines legislation, foreign takeovers having adverse competitive implications, with little or no offsetting justification based on efficiencies, should be prohibited. As a minimum, takeovers which (a) significantly reduce domestic competition; (b) reduce export opportunities for Canadian firms; (c) extend market dominance from abroad into Canada or otherwise increase or maintain market concentration; and (d) integrate a Canadian firm into an international cartel or curtail the vigour of Canadian competiton by placing the Canadian firm into an international pattern of concentration, ought to be prohibited.

In each case, if the acquisition would increase efficiency to the benefit of the Canadian market, the acquisition would not offend the Combines legislation. The purchase of a viable Canadian firm by a foreign firm, without adding any capacities which will make the firm more efficient, is of no advantage to Canada. If such a merger has any of the adverse effects set out above it is harmful to Canadian interests in competition and efficiency.

Aside from the role for Combines legislation in connection with mergers, the competitive impact of new foreign investment is a further aspect of the potential benefit or cost to the Canadian economy from foreign investment. Just as a foreign takeover might make a previously ineffective firm more competitive and innovative, new foreign investment could add considerably to the domestic competitive environment. In fact, it is possible that in some industries only foreign investment can be expected to add new suppliers to the domestic market in view of the barriers to entry which only an established firm can overcome. This could be due to capital costs of entry (the foreign firm might have internally available funds, superior credit worthiness in Canada, and easier access to foreign capital markets); the importance of some distinctive advantage (perhaps a degree of product differentiation of its own to rival present producers); or the economies of scale of some functions which only international markets for the spreading of certain costs can support. Truncated entry is possible for such a firm — expanding the scope of its Canadian activities as its market expands. The new entrant might, also, be less likely to participate in the local "business norms" which constrain competition.

The foreign entrant, in addition to stimulating competition in his own industry might also stimulate improved performance from suppliers in attempting to improve his own margin of profit — and possibly by instructing suppliers and related industries in techniques not formerly used by them.

As noted, however, foreign investment has historically not always added to the competitive vigour of the Canadian market. Foreign takeovers are more likely than new investment to reduce competition — and the acquisition by a foreigner of a dominant Canadian firm is more likely than a foreign acquisition of a smaller firm to restrict competition. The competitive impact of a new foreign investment which adds no new technology or efficiencies to Canada, can be equally adverse. Such entry can constitute a technique for extending domination in the Canadian market and achieving the restrictions set out above with regard to takeovers. Consequently, a screening procedure would have to bear in mind these aspects of foreign investment.

TAX AVOIDANCE

It is reasonable for international enterprises to arrange their affairs to minimize their tax burden on the total corporate venture. It is equally legitimate for host governments to ensure themselves of a fair share of tax revenues based on the income derived from business activity.

The principal concern in this regard relates to the prices on goods and services and other charges between affiliated firms whereby taxable income can be shifted out of Canadian tax revenues. The law on this point is, in principle, sufficient. Enforcement of all tax provisions is necessarily short of a complete audit of all taxpayers. Steps have been taken to examine more closely the issue of transfer prices.

Tax policy is frequently employed as a device for influencing the allocation of funds and resources within an economy. There are several aspects of significance for the filling of "gaps" in Canadian capacities and important issues for the differential in opportunities for Canadian and foreign controlled enterprises operating in Canada. Many of these have been considered in the context of the current tax reforms. However, the resulting tax policy cannot be expected to affect significantly the forces leading to foreign investment in Canada.

Transfer Pricing

In the absence of any controls on actual capital flows, the reassessment of transfer prices on goods or services between affiliated companies affects only the tax revenues of the host and home governments. The companies involved remain free to move funds as they see fit subject only to this constraint of paying the appropriate taxes.

The taxable profits of a Canadian firm can be made to vary dramatically by means of ostensibly minor changes in transfer prices. The tax revenues resulting from a foreign investment can be an important part of the benefits received by the host jurisdiction. These revenues are drawn out by the host government before the home government taxes the proceeds on repatriation. So long as the tax levels in the host jurisdiction are not above those of the home jurisdiction, and provided the home government permits the taxpayer to take credit for taxes paid to a foreign government, the taxpayer does not lose anything by the payment of taxes in the host economy. Where, however the total taxes in the host jurisdiction (income taxes plus withholding taxes on transfers) exceed those in the home country, the foreign investor incurs a heavier total tax bill. While the Canada-U.S. relative tax position is often one of higher taxes in Canada at the present time, the MNE can frequently absorb the higher Canadian taxes against the tax credit on other foreign income which is taxed below its home level in the United States.

The potential impact of taxable income from a relatively minor change in the transfer price can be illustrated by a simple example:

	A	B
Transfer price into Canada	$10.00	$10.50
Selling price in Canada	12.00	12.00
Gross profits in Canada	2.00	1.50
Local expenses in Canada	1.00	1.00
Net profit per unit	$ 1.00	$ .50

An increase of 5 per cent in the transfer price charged to the subsidiary reduces by 50 per cent the taxable income in Canada . . .

Other Techniques for Reducing Tax Revenues

Tax avoidance techniques are engaged in by all corporations regardless of whether they are Canadian or foreign controlled. There are very few that have special significance for foreign controlled firms that have not been dealt with under existing tax law or the proposed revisions. Brief mention should be made, however, of two other techniques.

"Thin capitalization" — the practice of an investor of placing an excessive portion of his investment capital in the form of debt rather than equity — permits the deduction of interest charges and the distribution of subsequent profits in the guise of a return of loan capital. When the transaction spreads over a national border, Canadian tax revenues are more seriously affected.

While thin capitalization can impair the ability of the corporation involved to raise further debt from outsiders, the foreign controlled subsidiary may find its credit worthiness rests ultimately with the parent firm. As a result, there would be fewer constraints on thin capitalization.

A second technique is that of the 5 per cent rate for deemed interest under Section 19(1) and related provisions under Section 8 of the Income Tax Act through which international enterprises can minimize their Canadian tax burden and facilitate the transfer of funds from the Canadian affiliate to other countries to meet corporate objectives. Section 19(1) provides for deemed interest at a rate of 5 per cent where an intercompany loan for other than business purposes is outstanding for more than 1 year. No interest need be charged if the loan is for less than a year.

If the Canadian corporation is able to borrow funds in Canada in a fashion which is tax deductible and to lend the money abroad at a low interest rate, the Canadian taxpayer is not sharing as much income from the loan as he might, and may also be subsidizing the foreign affiliate if the interest costs are deductible by the Canadian firm.

These transactions may facilitate the financing of international operations of non-Canadian firms at the expense of Canadian tax revenues. The revenues which are involved in this kind of transaction are probably not, however, very significant. The displacement of Canadian borrowers from the use of such funds is also probably minor. This matter is technically covered by Canadian tax law in that borrowing for this purpose is not deductible in Canada, but its tracing is difficult. This kind of tax avoidance is a more general problem in that Canadian taxpayers attempt to deduct interests costs on funds not strictly used for earning taxable income, although not, thereby, subsidizing a foreign affiliate.

Customs law and procedures generally are biased toward high import prices reflecting their concern with safeguarding the level of protection Parliament affords to Canadian producers to encourage Canadian production, employment and development generally regardless of ownership considerations. At the same time, this policy can have an adverse effect on the benefits accruing to Canada from the operation of foreign owned subsidiaries in terms of reducing the taxable base of these firms, facilitating transfers of profits to other jurisdictions and increasing the level of Canadian production costs via higher import prices.

BALANCE OF PAYMENTS IMPACT OF FOREIGN DIRECT INVESTMENT

To determine fully the long term impact of a foreign direct investment on the Canadian balance of payments requires that one trace through a series of direct and indirect consequences. Some efforts have been made to do this, but thus far this research does not permit precise quantification of the relationships. The best study available suggests that U.S. direct investments in Canada, on the average, have an aggregate deficit impact on the Canadian balance of payments after a period in excess of 10 years.

If through a period of time, it were demonstrated that the balance of payments consequences of direct investment in Canada were substantially more adverse in some sectors of the economy than in others, this might be reason to have some degree of bias against additional direct investment in that sector.

Direct investment in Canada often results in restrictions upon the export and import patterns of the Canadian subsidiary and in their freedom to purchase various kinds of services. These forced or contractual arrangements create, in the short-run, a 'locked-in' effect on the balance of payments. The result is that it is likely to be more difficult to use aggregate economic policies to get the kind of response in the current account which may be desirable at a certain point in time. This can complicate short-term decision making and thus provide yet another reason for seeking to minimize arbitrary restrictions on subsidiaries.

THE IMPACT OF CERTAIN FOREIGN LAWS AND POLICY ON THE BEHAVIOUR OF CANADIAN FIRMS – EXTRATERRITORIALITY

Introduction

Foreign laws and policies can affect Canadian firms in four basic kinds of circumstances.

Where the Canadian firm is part of an international structure and an affiliate located in a foreign jurisdiction is instructed to behave in a manner which affects the Canadian firm. This can occur where the firm is Canadian controlled or foreign controlled. For example, the U.S. Balance of Payments Policy affecting the flow of funds out of the United States.

Where a Canadian firm's affiliate in a foreign jurisdiction is instructed to require the Canadian firm to do or refrain from doing certain things. This too can affect Canadian controlled and foreign controlled firms. For example:

a. U.S. Balance of Payments Policy instructing a U.S. firm to have funds transferred from its Canadian subsidiaries;

b. the application of U.S. antitrust decrees against a U.S. firm, or a Canadian firm having a U.S. subsidiary, instructing that it have the Canadian firm comply;

c. the Trading with the Enemy Act prohibitions against firms controlled by U.S. persons or firms dealing with certain countries.

Where a Canadian firm having no international affiliation is obliged to accept certain conditions arising from international transactions. For example:

a. the restriction of re-exports of U.S. origin goods or technology from Canada under the Export Controls Act;

b. the impact of U.S. securities regulations might also fall into this category.

Where a Canadian corporation having no international corporate affiliation or transactions with the jurisdiction involved is directed to refrain from certain activities. For example, the Trading with the Enemy Act prohibition against U.S. nationals dealing with the nationals of certain countries.

Canada's exposure to these problems is considerable by virtue of the high degree of foreign investment and international commercial transactions – particularly with the U.S. As a matter of principle,

Canada has a right to exercise full control over activities which occur within its borders — and should assert this right. The direction of behaviour within Canada by foreign governments offends this principle. However, full assertion of this territorial sovereignty cannot get at some policies of foreign governments — i.e. those aimed at firms or persons in their jurisdiction and affecting their domestic activities. This exercise of authority can then affect the activities which might otherwise have gone on in Canada. Only a reduced exposure for Canada or international negotiations can neutralize these latter effects — although they may be of considerably greater economic significance to Canada (e.g. U.S. Balance of Payments Policies).

Trading with the Enemy Act

THE LEGISLATION

Any exportation or trading with Cuba. China, North Korea and North Vietnam is subject to prohibition when undertaken by persons subject to the jurisdiction of the U.S. courts. Section 5(b) of the Trading with the Enemy Act of 1917 empowers the President or his nominee "during the time of war or during any other period of national emergency declared by the President" to investigate, regulate or prohibit all commercial and financial transactions by Americans with certain foreign countries or the nationals of such countries.

APPLICATION OF THIS LEGISLATION

Aside from regulations under the Export and Import Permits Act, which require permits for the *re-export* of goods generally, and restrict the movement of strategic goods (these provisions on export controls are discussed next in this section), trade with the countries covered by this U.S. legislation is neither prohibited nor subject to licensing under Canadian law. In applying the Canadian law which requires licensing of re-exports from the country, Canada has undertaken to prevent the re-export of U.S. goods where the U.S. regulations prevent initial export.

POLICY ALTERNATIVES

Some sympathy might be expressed for U.S. attempts to enforce its law against blatant violations by Americans setting up non-operating firms in Canada solely to circumvent its rules. The law here has restricted Canadian activity based largely, or even purely, on Canadian commodities, technology and manufacture. This raises very different issues. The high degree of U.S. control of Canadian business creates a particularly high vulnerability to this sort of U.S. influence. If, however, the U.S. persists in penalizing persons over whom their courts have jurisdiction for such transactions — and if those persons have effective authority over firms operating in Canada — the alternatives for a Canadian policy which seeks to repel this extraterritorial influence (short of severing the links with the U.S. parent) are:

a. impose penalties on persons operating the Canadian firm over whom Canadian courts can exercise jurisdiction;

b. attempt to force the sale by confiscating or purchasing the goods under mandatory provisions and resell them to the buyer in the prohibited market; and

c. protest with the U.S. in an attempt to influence a revision of its rules.

The prohibition of refusals by Canadian firms to enter into export transactions, by virtue of the law of a foreign jurisdiction, is embodied in the revised Combines Act. This prohibitive approach has some value for particular proven instances. It cannot, however, be expected to deal generally with the problem.

The forcing of a sale through a governmental purchase of the goods in question could be considered as a general policy or as one which would arise as a specific performance remedy to cases found under (a) above to have violated the new Combines Act provisions.

It would be awkward for the Government however, to have to involve itself this directly and to have to assume the business risks of the transaction. Furthermore. while the prohibitive approach of the Combines Act sets out Government policy, it limits the offence to a refusal to deal by virtue of the foreign law only. A refusal based upon the marketing strategy of the firm would not be an offence. The Government might not be able to accept this as readily in circumstances where a Crown Agency is the ultimate selling body.

The lodging of a protest with the U.S. over this issue would be a renewal of earlier complaints and might be made to appear as a request by Canada for a "concession" rather than as an assertion of an authority over business taking place in Canada. This could give rise to public criticism of this approach. Furthermore, if the

U.S. were to make modifications, there might be a tendency to exact, however subtly, a reciprocal consideration from Canada — perhaps in other aspects of the foreign ownership policy which are of considerably greater economic and social significance for the country. This could occur despite the fact of a U.S. policy which is moving in the direction of liberalizing trade with China for reasons independent of Canadian governmental or public opinion. In fact, it is highly unlikely that the U.S. Government would change its policy on this matter because of Canadian pressures — although it might portray it that way to Canadian authorities, once decided upon for other reasons, if Canadian pressure were to be applied now.

The proposed screening process would, in the ordinary course of its examination, be identifying the export restrictions or opportunities available to a particular foreign controlled firm. The fact of export restrictions — whether arising from corporate policy or foreign law — (including restrictions arising from balance of payments policies of other countries) would constitute a disadvantage which would be included in the assessment. Non-U.S. firms would, in some industries, tend to receive a more favourable reception if they were subject to fewer such restrictions. Both the possibility of an ultimately lesser reliance on U.S. control in many industries and the disfavour of the screening authorities for export restrictions would lead to the exploration of other sources for investment or inputs. This might reduce the adverse impact of these provisions on Canadian trade — and potentially cause some pressure to be put on U.S. authorities by corporations seeking to operate in the Canadian market. This would not, however, serve to alter the impact of the presently high degree of foreign control of Canadian industry.

Conclusions

The assertion of jurisdiction over Canadian business and trade by the Government has certain symbolic value. The Combines approach is a partial step, but will not cover many of the impediments to trade with certain countries. The screening authorities would, similarly, not affect much of the prevailing impact of foreign law in this area.

The probability of trade with countries toward which Canadian policy does not discourage trade (at least in non-strategic goods) is the most politically offensive of the examples of extraterritoriality. It permits constraints, under some circumstances, despite 100 per cent Canadian content of the goods involved. Although the economic significance is not likely too great — particularly if trade with China in non-strategic goods becomes possible through U.S. controlled subsidiaries — the political impact is significant. The public may well be expecting some assertion of sovereignty on this matter in a foreign ownership policy. If the U.S. regulations regarding China approximate those affecting trade with the USSR and Eastern Europe, a unilateral Canadian assertion may not cause any serious reactions from the U.S. The prevailing Canadian sentiment and growing American public opinion could be of some assistance in acting on this issue at the present time.

Export Controls

THE LEGISLATION

The U.S. Department of Commerce, through its Office of Export Control, exercises authority under the Export Administration Act of 1969 (the somewhat liberalized successor to the legislation begun as the Export Control Act of 1947) to require licences of different kinds for all exports of commodities and technical data. Canada is basically exempt from this requirement for imports which are *destined for use or consumption in this country.* This treatment by the U.S. is unique.

Goods exported to Canada from the U.S. for re-export are subject to essentially the same restrictions as exports directly from the U.S. to those various export points. In the case of exports which can move from the U.S. under "general licence", re-exports of U.S. goods from Canada can proceed without securing any further American clearance. In the case of certain goods and technical data destined for designated countries which require "validated licences" (i.e. specific authorization for each export order based on declared destination), the approval of the Office of Export Control is technically required. (The Canadian authorities, however, under Canadian regulations requiring permits for re-exports basically apply the U.S. rules. If there is reason to believe that the Office of Export Control might not be in accord with such an export, the authorization of that Office is sought or a Canadian permit is refused.

Basically, these regulations apply to exports to communist countries — excluding Yugoslavia.

Generally, the U.S. provisions are easing over time but they are still significantly different from those of Canada. Furthermore, their rules regulating re-exportation from Canada apply beyond the practice of direct transhipment of goods in their original form. The

U.S. follows components and technical data (either embodied in commodities or separately) through levels of reassembly and manufacture in Canada in order to control their re-exportation.

The rules regarding re-export are technically binding on "any person" regardless of citizenship or residence, and regardless of the legality of the acts in question in the jurisdiction of their occurrence. Fines and imprisonment are provided for, but administrative sanctions are most common. The basic penalty is the rather severe economic sanction of an "order of denial of export privilege." U.S. exporters are denied the privilege of exporting and foreign importers are denied the opportunity of participating in export transactions from the U.S. — i.e. U.S. exporters are prohibited from dealing with such persons.

Canada has rules of its own which reflect strategic considerations, and its cooperation with the U.S. as a condition of securing free access to goods and technology from U.S. sources.

APPLICATION OF THIS LEGISLATION

Areas of conflict between the administration of the Canadian rules and those of U.S. do exist — and U.S. authorities would, in such cases, apply their rules directly.

Canadian controls apply to commodities and to technical data in a physical form (e.g. technical drawings) which have a value of over $50.00. No attempt is made in Canada to control the export of technical data or know-how in the minds of skilled personnel. The American rules do purport to cover such exportation. In this area the U.S. rules would apply directly since Canada does not require re-export permits. (Technical data which are "published" or generally available to the public are not subject to this set of controls in either country. Patented technology is regarded as being "published".)

The enforcement of this provision has been extended by the U.S. authorities to include U.S. "know-how" contained in the minds of U.S. citizens, acquired lawfully when applied in employment outside the United States. This would cover U.S. citizens working in research and development work for a firm in Canada — regardless of whether that firm was U.S.-owned or controlled.

A further area for direct application of U.S. controls would emerge when U.S. components are involved in Canadian manufactured goods. Canada exempts from control the re-export of goods (excluding the strategic category of commodities) which, despite being of non-Canadian origin, "have been further processed or manufactured in Canada, by combining them with other goods or otherwise, so as to result in a substantial change in value, form and use of the goods or in the production of new goods. . . ." There is scope for differing views between Canadian and American authorities as to whether the original national identity has been lost. If the U.S. Government rejects a Canadian view under which Canadian goods would not require a permit, the U.S. authorities may claim the applicability of their rules with consequent sanctions such as "blacklisting" of the Canadian manufacturer involved.

The point at which U.S. national identity is lost in the eyes of American authorities is unclear. If a component is used, in fact, the final commodity is subject to U.S. controls regardless of the minor nature of the component in the completed item. Similarly, the mixing of U.S.-sourced technology with Canadian or other know-how is not necessarily regarded by the U.S. Office of Export Controls as destroying its national origin.

Where there is no re-exportation involved, and the commodity is not otherwise restricted under the Canadian Export Control List, no licence is required by Canadian law. Exports of Canadian goods to Cuba, for example, would not have to be licensed — nor otherwise notified to Canadian authorities. If, however, some re-exportation of U.S. goods is involved, Canadian authorities would refuse to issue a licence for a sale to Cuba. If Canadian authorities were to feel that no re-exportation was involved in a particular case, they would not act to prevent the transaction.

The extensive reliance of Canadian industry on U.S. origin goods and technology creates substantial scope for the application of these re-exportation provisions. The fact of substantial U.S. control of Canadian manufacturing, and the revealed propensities of Canadian subsidiaries of U.S. parent firms to import from parents and their home economy, expand the scope of goods and technology whose re-exportation is subject to licensing and perhaps restricted. In either case, the U.S. trade policy determines export policy from Canadian firms in such circumstances. This applies to both foreign controlled and Canadian controlled firms securing components and technology from the United States.

While most countries exercise some control over the export of strategic goods and related technological data the United States has traditionally used its international trade policy for the broader purposes of its international policy. Based on its strength as an exporter of commodities and know-how, the U.S. has attempted to put at an economic disadvantage those countries towards which it is hostile. To enforce this policy, the U.S. has prevented U.S. exporters and foreign importers (whether U.S.-controlled or independent) from using foreign locations for the purpose of transhipping U.S.-origin goods and technology.

The economic significance of the constraints imposed by U.S. export controls cannot be readily assessed. Information regarding the frequency of refusals of export permits and the volume of trade thereby affected has not been collected by the Canadian authorities. Furthermore, the trade impact of voluntary compliance or persuasive enforcement by U.S. authorities which never comes to the attention of the government goes unrecorded. The total trade constraint which emerges from these controls and the extent of additional export trade in manufactured goods which might otherwise occur from Canada are matters for speculation at the present time.

There are a number of individual examples where U.S. Export Control Regulations have impeded Canadian exports — e.g. sale of an oil gathering system to the USSR; sale of a heavy water plant to Roumania; the sale of a microwave system to Czechoslovakia. As in the case of the Foreign Assets Control Regulations there are likely many cases which do not even come to light because the subsidiary is aware of the likely reaction of the U.S. Government.

There are two economic issues at stake — free and easy access to U.S. components and technology for domestic manufacturing and markets; and opportunity for Canadian manufacturing (Canadian or foreign controlled) to pursue export markets constrained only by Canadian international trade policy. Although this legislation has not been a subject of wide public debate in Canada, there is the political and symbolic issue of the constraints imposed on activities in Canada through U.S. policies.

In the final analysis, a determined U.S. Government can attach whatever conditions it wishes to exports from its industry. Even in the absence of Canadian cooperation, the U.S. could simply deny exports to Canada unless adequate assurances were made against offensive re-export. Whether the U.S. would be prepared to forego access to Canadian markets, what the nature of pressures from U.S. firms having Canadian subsidiaries would be in Washington and what the tone of U.S. public opinion would be on this issue if Canada were to move against such restrictions is not clear. How serious a denial of access to U.S. goods and technology would be for Canadian manufacturers and consumers, in view of alternative sources of such inputs, is not clear either. The most certain solution of this problem is, of course, a reduction of Canadian dependence on U.S.-origin components and technology.

Conclusions

The Combines Act revisions will have only a minimal effect on this aspect of the extraterritorial impact of U.S. laws. The repeal of Canadian re-export provisions is possible — but on the assumption that the U.S. would continue to control trade in its goods and technology, this step would simply complicate trade between Canada and the U.S. with no effect on the extent and nature of the export restrictions involved.

While attempting to reduce the impact of the restrictions through indigenous development and more diversified international sourcing of goods and technology, continued efforts should be made to have the U.S. modify its application of the rules regarding the transformation of goods by Canadian manufacturing.

In the final analysis, the U.S. is active only within its own jurisdiction when it seeks to control the outflow of goods and technology from its industry. It is when it also impinges on Canadian goods and technology that it enters the field of extraterritoriality. However, the economic impact of its policy is felt in Canada even before it reaches this more technical sense of extraterritoriality.

Antitrust

THE LEGISLATION

The American antitrust legislation specifically acknowledges the application of its principles of freedom for American traders from any restraint on foreign commerce. U.S. firms must not be denied access to world markets by arbitrary corporate action, nor is the U.S. domestic market to be denied the benefits of the competitive pressures from any potential sources for imports. Section 1 of the Sherman Act, for example, makes illegal "Every contract, combination . . . or conspiracy, in restraint of trade or commerce among the several States, or with foreign nations. . . ."

THE APPLICATION OF THIS LEGISLATION

To pursue this objective of prohibiting restrictions on either the export or import trade of the United States, the administration of the Sherman and Clayton Acts (the two basic statutes affecting conspiracies or agreements and mergers) has involved the assertion by the U.S. of jurisdiction over activities which have occurred outside the country but which have affected domestic or international trade markets of U.S. business.

Canada has experienced the impact of the extraterritorial extensions by the U.S. courts in antitrust matters in three basic ways. The U.S. courts have asserted direct jurisdiction over persons and firms in Canada (i.e. actually made such persons defendants in antitrust suits). The U.S. courts have attempted to secure evidence which was held in the files of Canadian companies. The decrees following a conviction of a Canadian defendant or a U.S. defendant have directed that specific corrective measures be taken in Canada or that the offensive behaviour cease.

These extraterritorial assertions over foreign business conduct only emerged in the post World War II period. Prior to that time the U.S. courts had operated under the assumption that all legislation was *prima facie* intra-national. This reflects, in part, the advance of activity through international business structures and transactions which could readily frustrate the purposes of U.S. antitrust policy. Blatant circumvention of a domestic policy becomes possible under such circumstances – either through foreign firms set up for that purpose of incidentally used to achieve results not available through domestic action.

The U.S. courts have paid only limited attention to the policy of the host environment affected by a decree.

Since 1959 an agreement has existed between Canada and the U.S. – the "Antitrust Notification and Consultation Procedure" – providing that each government "in enforcing its own antitrust or anti-combines laws, consults the other when it appears that the interests of the other country will be affected by such enforcement." This is not a condition precedent to a suit, and does nothing to protect foreign conduct which is unlawful under U.S. legislation. The U.S. has seemingly modified its approach only to the extent of naming foreign participants as co-conspirators rather than as direct defendants. The legal liability then attaches only to the U.S. national and relies on the control of the foreign subsidiary to effect behaviour abroad in compliance with a decree.

Unilateral steps have been taken by some governments in response to the extraterritorial application of U.S. antitrust law. The major focus of legislative reaction against these activities of U.S. antitrust laws has been in the area of documentation. In preparing a case, U.S. authorities have attempted to secure information on foreign activities which is often in the hands of foreign firms. The U.S. has attempted to summon documents from U.S.-owned pulp and paper subsidiaries. In response, Ontario passed its Business Records Protection Act in 1950 prohibiting the removal of corporate records from Ontario where such removal "would be consistent with compliance with any requirement, order, direction or subpoena of any legislative, administrative or judicial authority in any jurisdiction outside Ontario. . . ." In 1958, Quebec passed similar legislation in its Business Concerns Records Act.

The two provincial enactments in Canada do not provide for governmental consent and do not prohibit disclosure on a "voluntary" basis by companies within the two jurisdictions. In fact, two Canadian firms were "requested" to reply to questionnaires sent by the U.S. Department of Justice (Antitrust Division). This preceded any legal action and was related to assessing the adequacy of the evidence for the instituting of an action. It would appear that the Fulton-Rogers Agreement of 1959 and the Basford-Mitchell Agreement of 1969 would not *require* notification of Canadian authorities by either Canadian companies or U.S. authorities. (It appears nevertheless, that an Aide-Memoire was sent on April 14, 1964 to inform the Canadian authorities that these questionnaires were to be sent to the two companies.)

POLICY ALTERNATIVES

In the absence of some positive move by Canada, the U.S. authorities and courts will continue to pursue their statutory mandate to protect U.S. domestic and export markets from the anti-competitive acts of companies.

Under present judicial interpretation and U.S. legislation, it is open to Canada to "occupy" the field of competition policy by directing certain acts, prohibiting others, and constraining acts in compliance with foreign decrees to circumstances where it is considered to be compatible with Canadian interests. Furthermore, the effective implementation of a Canadian competition policy also requires that account be taken of international business structures and activities. The revised Combines Act will deal with most of these problems of extraterritorial application of foreign law and of the effective implementation of a Canadian policy on competition in a manner which will be set out below.

CONCLUSIONS

American antitrust enforcement has involved a more direct form of extraterritoriality than the areas of policy discussed earlier. In protecting its policy aimed at preserving market forces, the U.S. has asserted jurisdiction over activities which occurred outside the U.S. on the grounds that they have adversely affected domestic or international trade markets of U.S. business. Canada has experienced the impact of the decrees of U.S. courts in several cases.

The new Combines Act does, however, respond to most of these issues. The addition of a foreign takeover rule and the restricting of the summoning of documents by foreign authorities would complete the policy response to the concerns set out in this section.

Securities

THE LEGISLATION

U.S. securities legislation aims at the protection of Americans in their investment activities. In view of the openness of U.S. and Canadian financial markets, a good deal of portfolio investment exists over the border with Americans investing in Canadian companies. These investments are occasionally made in the U.S. but are for the financing of Canadian corporate ventures. Furthermore, Americans could frustrate U.S. securities policy by using a Canadian corporate framework to evade the substantive provisions of U.S. law while raising funds for a corporate venture in the U.S. This policy does, however, create situations in which Canadians find themselves directed to comply with American rules — even under circumstances where they do not themselves seek to appeal to U.S. investors for funds.

The Canadian Government proposed that Canadian companies that wished to have access to the U.S. over-the-counter market be subject to the same rules as non-North-American issuers (the SEC having provided somewhat easier rules for them due to the lower incidence of investment activity in such companies by Americans), and that Canadian companies that did not wish access to the market be given a complete exemption from the rules. The U.S. Government did not accept Canadian representations to the effect that the application of the rules be limited to Canadian companies deliberately seeking access to the U.S. market.

To some extent, the superior level of protection offered in the U.S. on such matters as securities distribution is the root of the problem, and the principle of territorial sovereignty aside, the substance of the U.S. provisions is often quite attractive and a useful prod to Canadian policy on the subject matter involved. It is precisely the policy differences between Canada and some foreign jurisdiction – principally the U.S. – which creates these conflicts of extraterritoriality. However, it is also on these grounds that the question of whose public policy is to take dominance is focused. It would presumably be open to the U.S. to handle this matter by prohibiting dealers from trading in issues which do not meet the SEC standards. Then no extraterritorial effect would exist and only Canadians voluntarily submitting to the jurisdiction of the SEC would be affected by its rules.

POLICY ALTERNATIVES

The extraterritoriality involved in the holding of Canadian corporations and individuals liable for violations of other provisions of the U.S. securities regulations is similarly not readily subject to easy solution by unilateral Canadian action. When American shareholders are affected by actions taking place entirely in Canada, the attempt by the SEC to hold the Canadian corporation or individuals involved liable in damages appears, on its face, to be somewhat more offensive. Nevertheless, so long as these prohibitions and penalties cannot be enforced in Canada (a matter entirely within the jurisdiction of the Canadian Government) there is, strictly speaking, no extraterritoriality involved. If American policy finds particular activities to be unlawful, Canadian legislation cannot repel decisions from impeding the Canadian corporations or individuals from ready access to U.S. capital markets nor prevent the imposition of penalties on any holdings which these corporations or individuals have in the U.S.

CONCLUSIONS

These aspects of extraterritoriality have not received much public attention. The economic impact which they have had would not seem to approach that of the areas of trade policy or antitrust legislation. Similarly, they cannot be seen to have seriously impinged on economic activity or business structures within Canada. As a result, a legislative declaration against these rules would not seem to be meaningful.

U.S. Balance of Payments Programme

INTRODUCTION

The United States has experienced balance of payments deficits throughout the past two decades. These deficits initially served a useful purpose in relieving the acute dollar shortage in the rest of

he world after the war. But as they continued, the weakening U.S.
dollar became a source of growing concern, and a series of measures
has been undertaken by the U.S. Government to deal with the
situation. For most of the period, the U.S. earned a substantial
surplus on current account, and the overall deficit arose from the
fact that the outflows of private U.S. capital and U.S. Government
expenditures abroad for military purposes and for aid have been
larger than current earnings.

The measures taken by the U.S. to restore balance were thus
primarily directed at reducing the net outflow of capital and easing
the foreign exchange cost of the Government's overseas programmes.
They have produced results, but the problem has since been com-
pounded by a decline in the current account surplus itself, so that
the overall deficits have risen to even higher levels. Accordingly,
U.S. policy has placed greater emphasis on measures to restore the
trade surplus to its former levels, while maintaining the programme
of capital restraints.

IMPACT ON CANADA

The announcement of the U.S. Interest Equalization Tax in
July 1963 caused immediate and serious problems for Canada.
Heavy selling pressure developed against the Canadian dollar. The
reserves dropped sharply, causing the Government to seek and to
obtain an exemption from the IET for United States purchases of
new issues of Canadian securities. This principle of exempting
Canada was maintained throughout the successive elaborations of
the U.S. balance of payments programme. Canada's current account
balance was in large and chronic deficit. A very large current deficit
with the U.S. was only partly covered by the current surplus with
other countries and Canada's resulting needs for capital inflows could
only be met in the U.S. Capital inflows took the form of direct
investment and of fixed interest borrowing by provinces, municipalities and corporations in the U.S. bond market. Since capital
imports from the U.S. were smaller than the current account deficit
with the U.S., Canada argued that it was not contributing to the
U.S. balance of payments deficit but rather helping to finance it.
Any restriction on Canadian borrowing in the U.S. could only be
offset by adjustments elsewhere in the balance of payments, such as
the trade account, which would inevitably affect the U.S. adversely.

These same arguments were employed in December 1965 to obtain an exemption from the U.S. Voluntary Programme when it
was extended to cover long-term investment by U.S. financial

institutions and direct investment by U.S. non-financial corporation Canada did not initially express great concern over the application of the U.S. mandatory controls on direct investment in Canada which were introduced on January 1, 1968. It was recognized that they were directed against Western Europe which had been accumulating large balance of payments surpluses. Furthermore, private investment in Canada of all kinds was expected to be lower in 1968 than in 1967 and direct investment from the U.S. had already fallen in 1967 to about the level that would be permitted in 1968 under the 65 per cent provision. Generally speaking, the advantages of avoiding any limitation on fixed interest borrowing in the U.S. were regarded as greater than the avoidance of any limitation on direct investment. Moreover, the administrative discretion given to companies to exceed their ceilings in special circum stances provided some reassurance that industries dependent on U.S. capital would not suffer unduly.

However, a series of developments, including the decline in wheat exports to the Soviet Union and China and the disturbances in the international monetary system at that time contributed to a new crisis for the Canadian dollar early in 1968. A substantial transfer of funds from Canadian subsidiaries to U.S. parent companies appeared to be taking place despite the announcement by the U.S. Government that such massive repatriation of liquid assets was not an objective of the U.S. Programme and that U.S. subsidiaries in Canada were expected to behave as good corporate citizens. Finally, on March 7, 1968, agreement was reached in which the U.S. undertook to exempt Canada from all the U.S. balance of payments measures affecting capital flows that were administered by the Department of Commerce or the Federal Reserve System.

In return for the exemptions from the IET and the Commerce a FRB programmes, Canada has given certain undertakings which are designed to assure the U.S. that undue use will not be made of the exemptions by Canada, and that they will not lead to an invasion of the restrictions affecting other countries by a movement of fund through Canada. At the time the original exemption from the IET was obtained in 1963, Canada undertook to ensure that funds woul not be borrowed in the U.S. in order to add to the official reserves of gold and foreign exchange. This implied a ceiling on the reserves at the level of $2,700 million which had been reached prior to the announcement of the IET, and this ceiling was maintained with some downward revision until December 17, 1968. In an exchange of letters of that date between the Minister of Finance and the Secretary of the U.S. Treasury, this ceiling was replaced by a more general understanding that it was not in Canada's interest to increase its reserves through unnecessary borrowing in the U.S. market. This recognized the fact that the IET had proved to be more long lasting than had originally been anticipated and that the expanding capital markets of other countries provided Canada with a means of achieving an increase in its reserves which would not be at the expense of the U.S.

Secondly, Canada issued a series of guidelines for banks (May 3, 1968), non-bank financial institutions (July 24 1968), and non-financial corporations (September 19, 1968), to ensure that unlimited access to the U.S. capital market by Canada would not result in by-passing the U.S. balance of payments guidelines. These guidelines did not aim to reduce Canadian foreign holdings, but they did seek to maintain them at their then current levels. As such, Canadian subsidiaries were not restricted from re-investing funds earned abroad; and Canadian individuals could invest in third countries, the only restriction being that they should not purchase "offshore" U.S. corporate bonds.

Canadian banks were asked not to increase their foreign currency claims on residents of countries other than Canada and the U.S. above the level held at the end of February 1968 unless this increase was accompanied by an equal increase in total foreign currency liabilities to residents of third countries. Non-bank financial institutions were asked to limit the increase in their foreign currency claims on residents of third countries to the level at the end of June 1968, unless the increase wholly represented liabilities to residents of third countries, or arose out of net earnings of foreign branches or subsidiaries. Non-financial corporations were not to increase their holdings of assets in Continental Western Europe in any way that involved a transfer of capital from the U.S. or Canada. Restraint was to be exercised in any investment in other countries and should in the first instance be of a nature that would improve Canada's trade and international payments position.

Thirdly, Canada agreed to invest the U.S. dollar portion of the official reserves in excess of working balances in special non-marketable Treasury securities. This served the purpose of reducing the U.S. balance of payments deficit on the liquidity basis but did not affect the deficit on the official settlements basis.

CONCLUSIONS

To the extent that the United States Programme applied to outflows of capital from the U.S., it did not involve extraterritorial application of that country's policy. On the other hand, in trying to influence the dividend policy and the import and export activity of foreign controlled U.S. firms, it was serving to transmit U.S. Government policy abroad through the network of parents and subsidiaries. That portion of the programme aimed at influencing the behaviour of foreign controlled firms thus did contain a measure of extraterritoriality.

The U.S. Programme did not apply to Canada following the Canadian requests for exemptions. In return for the exemptions, Canada has taken certain steps which have been of assistance to the U.S. The need to seek an exemption from the U.S. reflected the dependence of Canada on the U.S. arising from the current account deficits in the Canadian balance of payments. It reflected also some of the gaps in the Canadian capital markets.

In reaching these arrangements, a certain cost has been incurred by Canada. Its financial firms have been limited by the restrictions on capital exports. Much more importantly, during the period of the ceiling on exchange reserves, the choices available to the monetary authorities in regulating credit conditions were reduced. In particular, the level of interest rates had to take account of the need to minimize capital inflows. While the inflows could, up to a point, be offset by Canadian Government purchases of marketable U.S. securities when excess exchange reserves were being accumulated, this did not constitute an entirely satisfactory response. Thus the exchange reserve limitation involved some restriction on the use of monetary policy as an instrument to fight inflation.

With the elimination of the current account deficit, the balance of payments need for Canada's exemptions from the U.S. programmes is no longer present. The exemptions are still of some value, however, largely because certain Provincial and Municipal Governments may not be able to obtain all of the funds they need in the Canadian open market.

During most of the 1960's, the Canadian exemption from the U.S. programme reflected both the current account deficit and the inability of the Canadian capital market to mobilize the sums needed for some large borrowings and equity issues. If the U.S. programme had applied to Canada, it might in theory have been possible to apply exchange controls in order to prevent an acceleration of dividend payments or excessive business service charges from Canadian subsidiaries to their parents and more generally, to maintain the level of the exchange rate. But the problem would have remained that Canada's need for investment capital would not have been satisfied, at least initially, by the Canadian capital markets. Accordingly, it was difficult for Canada not to seek the exemptions.

With the elimination of the current account deficit, any future U.S. programme which might apply to Canada would be more tolerable from the viewpoint of the balance of payments. The need for investment capital, however, would remain. Thus, the primary need for Canada, in developing the capacity to resist any future extensions of U.S. balance of payments policy to Canada, is to obtain better entrepreneurship from the Canadian capital markets.

THE IMPACT OF FOREIGN CONTROL OF CANADIAN BUSINESS ON CANADIAN CULTURE AND SOCIETY

Introduction

This section examines the impact of the high degree of foreign control of Canadian business on Canadian culture and society. It begins with a consideration of cultural attitudes in Canada which have facilitated foreign direct investment. It goes on to consider the impact of foreign direct investment on the cultural and social environment. It concludes that there is a high degree of interaction between the above two factors but that the presence of large volumes of foreign investment concentrated in U.S. hands increases the difficulty of developing a distinctive Canadian culture. This has potentially serious implications since the economic and political strength of a country lie largely in the creation of a cultural, social and political milieu which favours indigenous initiative and innovation.

J.K. Galbraith has argued that Canadians should not worry about the concentrated U.S. ownership of Canadian business, but about maintaining the cultural integrity of the broadcasting system and making sure that Canada has an active, independent theatre, book publishing industry, newspapers, magazines, and schools of poets and painters. This reflects a rather naive view of culture and nationhood. There is no way of leaving the "economic" area to others, so that we can get on with the political, social and cultural concerns in our own way. There is no such compartmentalization in the real world. When culture is understood in this broad sense, there can be little doubt that economic activity, as organized in the modern corporation, has a profound impact on culture, especially on the nature of the social, political and economic system, and the technology employed.

Having indicated the complex inter-relationships within a culture, it is difficult to isolate and analyse the corporate impact, whether domestic or foreign, on culture. This is especially true in the case of Canada, since Canada is basically an open society and many influences have shaped Canadian culture and society. It is difficult, for example, to distinguish those aspects of our cultural and social development which are the effects of general industrial, technological and economic development and those which are foreign or U.S. importations and infiltrations. It is equally difficult to disentangle the influence of foreign control of Canadian business from the impact of a common language, the mass media, political tradition similar in numerous respects, the use of the same books at universities and at public schools, imports, travel, common professional associations and trade unions, and close family and friendship links. Of course, there is a feedback process involved and inter-corporate links between Canada and the U.S. reinforce some of these other relationships. In any event, it will always be difficult to determine whether a particular aspect of U.S. influence in Canada is related to corporate control or other types of cultural inter-relationships.

Countries of similar cultures and per capita real income appear to be particularly susceptible to direct investment. While there are some important differences between Canadian and U.S. culture (the bilingual and bicultural character of Canada; the republican form of government in the U.S.; the tolerance in Canada of a greater role for governmental action, such as the C.B.C., the railroads, and Air Canada; distinctive Canadian institutions such as the co-operative movement on the Prairies, the Caisses Populaires in Quebec, and the existence of socialist parties in Canada), the numerous and important cultural similarities facilitate direct investment.

A further factor which has facilitated foreign direct investment is that Canadians, by and large, are not very xenophobic. Canada has fewer national heroes and distinctive symbols than most other countries. Canadians seem to have less pride in their history and in their achievements. While British, American or French history is, in a certain sense, part of our own history, it is studied more assiduously than Canadian history. The reasons for this are very complex, but in part Canadian diffidence towards nationhood appears to arise out of Canada's colonial past. In more recent times, Canada's proximity to the dynamic and powerful U.S. has induced a comparable feeling of dependence or inferiority.

The lack of a strong national identity and a distinctive culture tend to create, as outlined above, a vacuum and a greater receptivity to foreign influence and investment. The ease of importing our culture from the U.K. or the U.S. reinforces this tendency by reducing the pressure on Canadians to develop their own cultural distinctiveness. On this fertile ground foreign investment has a relatively easy task in shaping and influencing the Canadian environment. Looked at from the point of view of the U.S. investor, the openness and lack of cultural distinctiveness reduce the risk and cost of foreign investment since there is less need to adapt the product locally. Thus, foreign investment at one and the same time plays on cultural similarities and reduces the capacity for the distinctive development of national identity.

It is interesting to consider the situation of Quebec in the light of this analysis. Quebec has a distinctive culture, largely the result of a different language and religious and educational institutions. French Canadians by and large are taught French Canadian history. They know their heroes and their symbols. The Government of Quebec is trying to retain and develop this culture through a number of policies, particularly those relating to language and education. These differences probably make Quebec a less attractive location for U.S. investment than Ontario. It is, of course, very difficult to determine whether the higher rate of U.S. investment in Ontario is the result of cultural similarity or the more rapid rate of economic growth that they have enjoyed in recent years.

The Impact of Foreign Direct Investment on Culture

In discussing the determinants of foreign direct investment in manufacturing, it was suggested that direct investment arises from the desire of a manufacturer to exploit in foreign markets some distinctive capacity developed by him for his domestic market. This distinctive advantage (whether it be technology, a differentiated product, marketing, financial or management skills) has been developed in a particular cultural milieu and embodies certain cultural values. These may be good or bad, but they exist. In the case of U.S. direct investment, the "cultural baggage" accompanying a particular investment embodies basically the "free enterprise tradition", both in terms of its values and its actual behaviour. The foreign investor naturally has little interest in developing distinctive Canadian capacities and in preserving the Canadian heritage.

Cultural Impact of Technology

Some of the less desirable aspects of what is often attributed to U.S. corporations should, in the opinion of some people, be attributed largely to the impact of modern technology. However, as pointed out above, it is for all practical purposes impossible to distinguish the impact of these two forces because they are almost always associated with each other. Technology is developed in a particular milieu and tends to reflect certain other cultural values;

for example, technology developed in the U.S. seems to place greater emphasis on rapid innovation and change and the satisfaction of peripheral wants which often have to be created than appears to be the case in Europe. This seems to be especially true in manufacturing sectors dominated by U.S. multinational companies. Compare the engineering and design and the rate of change in these two factors of a Chevrolet on the one hand and a Volkswagen or Volvo on the other.

This is not to say that Canada should opt out of technological society, but rather that if technology is in foreign hands it is likely that the use and adaptation of this technology to meet local cultural demands will be minimized. If technology is in Canadian hands, the chances are greater that its use will be adapted to the needs of the Canadian milieu.

Cultural Impact of Marketing Capacities

The large investments required in the creation of new technologies and new products means that corporation smust assure markets for them by spending vast amounts on advertising to create the wants and formulate the tastes, in the absence of which financial disaster could result.

The large investments required in the creation of new technologies and new products means that corporations must assure markets for them by spending vast amounts on advertising to create the the existence of advertising spill-over. A "product image" often exists in Canada even before a dollar is spent on advertising here.

Cultural Impact of Truncation

Since a significant number of foreign controlled companies operating in Canada lack some of the decision making powers and activities of a normal Canadian controlled business enterprise, their activities can be described as "truncated".

The exercise of vital entrepreneurial functions by the parent with the consequent truncation of entrepreneurial activities in the Canadian subsidiary has adverse effects, not only on Canadian economic development, but also on Canadian society in general. Truncation means less challenging jobs for the Canadian techno-structure which must frequently look to the U.S. for more challenging job opportunities: if you want to be on the ninety-fifth floor, with global horizons, you must go to New York; the highest one can go in Canada is the fifty-fourth floor. But the effects of truncation go beyond reducing the number of challenging jobs for the relatively small group of Canadian entrepreneurs and managers. The under-development of the Canadian techno-structure has adverse social and cultural effects in that the "spill-over" benefits resulting from the interaction of these "brains" takes place not in Canada, but abroad. Truncation also tends to engender a mentality of the second best with horizons and vision constantly centred on headquarters abroad. It represents a continuation of the colonial mentality described above. This attitude is manifested in many ways such as the preference for finishing a person's education by sending him to Oxford, Harvard, the London School of Economics or the Sorbonne. It is manifested in the difficulty of recruiting top quality foreigners for business or our universities because of the general view that the best opportunities exist not in Canada, but abroad where parent companies and other centres of decision are located. The general effects of truncation are vividly summed up in the phrase "branch plant mentality"

However, the effects of truncation are not the only operative forces in this situation; the fact that Canadian society is quite élitist and that social mobility is more circumscribed in Canada means that Canadian society is not developing entrepeneurs at the same rate as occurs elsewhere. Social rigidity induces the expectation and mentality of working for others.

Other Factors

The U.S. manager who often accompanies U.S. direct investment in Canada also has a considerable cultural impact as a member of the business élite. Having been born, educated and raised in the U.S., being familiar with the history, geography, and culture of that country, his impact is bound to reflect social and cultural values moulded in an American milieu. Often he brings with him a taste and preference for U.S. products and ways of doing things which go beyond the methods of doing business. His membership in American-based professional associations and clubs, his family and friendship links with the U.S., for example, will tend to reduce his identification with the Canadian community.

The cultural impact of foreign investment is magnified in part because of the sectoral distribution of this investment. There is high foreign control in industries which have considerable cultural impact such as book publishing, and in industries which are responsible for the dissemination of culture, such as film and book distribution. Foreign control and U.S. control in particular, is high in those industries in which taste formation, product innovation and differentiation are crucial, such as automobiles, pharmaceuticals, and electrical products. High foreign investment in the resource industries has less of an impact on culture because the purpose of the investment is basically extraction and export, and the resource industries employ and thus affect relatively fewer Canadians.

It is interesting to speculate whether the cultural impact of foreign corporate activity (including the possibility of creating a more distinctive Canadian culture) might not be decreased were foreign investment not so heavily concentrated in U.S. hands.

At present, the Canadian business community is largely Americanized, either because it consists of U.S. controlled firms or firms which have adopted U.S. business strategy and tactics to compete with U.S. firms. Might not a reduction in the preponderance of U.S. investment and the introduction of a greater diversity of sources of investment enhance the prospect of developing a distinctive Canadian identity? Such a policy of diversification would be consistent with the thrust of the screening process which advocates the search for better alternatives.

If Canadians are concerned about the development of a distinctive Canadian culture, the question arises whether the recommended policies on foreign investment will influence the situation. The impact on Canadian cultural development will probably only be marginal; it is no substitute for the development of specific cultural policies to foster the development of a stronger Canadian identity. Socio-cultural attitudes in Canada are evolving; in particular a new and more confident sense of nationhood seems to be developing. A foreign ownership policy could be regarded as one useful manifestation of this new nationhood.

THE IMPACT OF FOREIGN CONTROL ON THE POLITICAL PROCESS AND PUBLIC POLICY

A main difficulty in this task is in isolating the impact of the foreign controlled firm from the generally pervasive impact of American influence in Canada. On the one hand, much of the United States influence in Canada is due to factors other than U.S. investment. On the other hand, the investment does contribute to the general openness between the two countries, both in itself and by encouraging the continuing flow of trade, persons and ideas across the border.

In examining the impact of foreign control upon the political process and public policy, two factors are considered.

One is the political behaviour of the foreign controlled firm; for instance, its intervention in an election or its appearance before a Parliamentary Committee to support or to oppose a policy; or more subtly, its promotion of an image which it may find helpful in its dealings with Government (e.g. the current advertising expenditures of the mining association stressing the value of mining to the economy are no doubt related to that industry's concern about tax reform).

The second factor considered is the impact the foreign controlled firm has on the outputs or decisions of the political system and on Canada's political options. The fact that a foreign controlled firm may put great pressure on a Government certainly does not mean that the Government will knuckle under to it. Conversely, the fact that a foreign controlled firm may not intervene consciously and actively in the political process does not mean that the decision of the Government may not be limited by the fact that the firm is foreign controlled or that the choices facing the Government may not be limited by the overall high degree of foreign control. In short, the relationship between behaviour and impact is not necessarily direct.

Moreover, the overall political impact of extensive and concentrated foreign control can go beyond the capacity of particular foreign controlled firms to affect particular decisions. It may also help to shape or to limit the broad political choices available to Canada (at least in some aspects of policy) and the ability to achieve national ends.

The Behaviour of Foreign-Controlled Firms (Inputs)

Conceptually, it is possible to envisage a very wide range of methods through which foreign controlled firms might seek to influence the political system and policies of a host country. Several different degrees of possible intervention are considered below. The extent to which each is experienced in Canada is the question at issue.

A foreign controlled firm may act as the political agent of its home government and seek to overthrow or to maintain in power the host government to help advance the policy objectives of its home government. Conversely, the foreign controlled business may solicit the support of its home government to overthrow or to maintain the régime in the host country. At its most extreme, these possibilities may involve revolution or coup d'état.

While such intervention is clearly illegitimate, the practice is not unknown in the modern world. For instance, major international oil and mining companies have on occasion tried and succeeded in helping to overthrow or to prop up régimes in parts of Latin America and Africa.

However, there is no available evidence which would support the view that foreign controlled firms have either been enlisted by home governments or solicited the support of home governments to seek non-constitutional overthrow of the Canadian governmental system.

A less extreme version of the above would involve very active intervention of foreign controlled firms in Canadian general elections, either at the behest of its home government or at its own initiative.

With respect to elections, the formal organizations of the business community do not generally give open collective support to any one political party. Thus, while particular firms or businessmen may publicly support a political party, or contribute to one or more parties, such organizations as the Canadian Manufacturers' Association, the Canadian Chamber of Commerce, the Canadian Textiles Institute and the Canadian Chemical Producers' Association do not normally do so. In other words, foreign controlled firms obviously do not cloak their intervention in electoral politics by having the trade associations act on their behalf

Secondly, no evidence is available that would suggest that the behaviour of the individual foreign controlled firm differs in any significant way from that of the domestically controlled business firm in election campaigns; for instance, in its pattern of contribution to parties.

Another way in which the foreign controlled firm might influence the political process would be by responding to the directives or requests of its home government to influence host government public policy, e.g. if General Motors were to lobby the Government of Canada to give more active support to U.S. policy in Viet Nam. In practice, while there might be isolated illustrations of such behaviour, there is no evidence of this being a common activity.

A fourth method through which the foreign controlled firm can influence the political process is through its capacity to obtain the support of its home government (a foreign government) to uphold its interests in Canada. In the generality, the right of a home government to make these kinds of representations to the government of a country in which one of its firms has established a subsidiary is accepted as legitimate.

For the most part, once again little evidence has been found that foreign controlled firms have frequent recourse to such a method of protecting or advancing their interests. In part, this may be because there is little discrimination between foreign and Canadian controlled firms in Canadian law and public administration. And, of course, when a foreign government does seek to intervene on behalf of a subsidiary, it does not necessarily follow that it will be able to convince the host government to modify its position. The cases of the Mercantile Bank and Time-Reader's Digest are the two most obvious examples of foreign government pressure being brought to bear on the political process due to the fact that these firms were foreign controlled. Thus far, in respect of the divestiture rulings of the CRTC, there has been no substantial intervention by the U.S. authorities, possibly because the United States has broadcasting legislation not unlike Canada's.

This picture might be altered by more extensive Japanese investment in Canada. Unlike American and British investment, Japanese investment reflects the very close relationship between government and the private sector in that economy. If Japanese investment in Canada were to become very large, it is likely the Japanese Government would be quite active in protecting and advancing the investments of its nationals in Canada.

On the whole, however, this is once again a situation of only a few isolated cases. For the most part, foreign controlled firms have not introduced foreign governments into the Canadian political process.

Less directly, foreign controlled firms affect the nature of the advice which various levels of Government receive from the business community. Foreign controlled business firms play active roles in such trade associations as the Canadian Manufacturers' Association and the Canadian Chamber of Commerce. Indeed, they may constitute the main source of financial support for the CMA. Foreign controlled firms are also active in various formal and informal government advisory committees, such as the National Advisory Committee on Petroleum and the Business Advisory Committee of the Ministry of Industry, Trade and Commerce.

Western liberalism accepts that individuals and groups have a legitimate right to try to influence public policy and to secure redress from grievances by lawful collective action. Indeed, much public policy emerges out of the clash of conflicting group interests. It is further recognized in the liberal democratic political system that the business community is a participant in the political process, and that this is entirely proper, subject to appropriate traditional and legal limitations.

These facts take on a particular significance when viewed in the Canadian context. Many of the largest and most concentrated Canadian industries are dominated by foreign controlled firms and inevitably the policies and attitudes of these firms reflect those of their parent companies. That is, through the medium of subsidiary firms, some of the most important political pressures which are brought to bear upon the Canadian government from *within* the Canadian political system can reflect the interests of foreign businesses.

These facts do not, of course, constitute an indictment of the behaviour of foreign controlled firms. For one thing, the subsidiary doubtless sometimes expresses itself to the Canadian Government in much the same way as it would if it were Canadian controlled in that the parent firm does not have an interest significantly different than Canadian controlled businesses. Secondly, the subsidiary is a Canadian citizen under Canadian law, and thus entitled to the political right of making representations to the Government . Indeed, it is recognized that good corporate citizenship is by no means restricted to Canadian controlled firms nor bad citizenship to foreign controlled enterprises. Thirdly, the Government normally has a continuing need for information from business. If the firms in a sector which is largely dominated by foreign controlled enterprises were unwilling to come to Ottawa and to talk, needed information might not be available to the Government. This, of course, by no means pre-supposes that the information or advice from business is accepted uncritically.

Thus, it is not a criticism of the individual foreign controlled firm to observe that it can at times serve as a vehicle for foreign corporate influence within the Canadian political system. However, there are around 8,000 such firms in Canada, almost 4,000 are U.S. controlled and many of these are amongst Canada's largest firms. The cumulative impact of their normal political activities thus gives the U.S. corporate view a very important voice in the Canadian political arena. Accordingly, the views expressed by Canadian industry will be heavily influenced by U.S. business interests.

For instance, in trying to rationalize the structure of the rubber tire and chemical industries, it seems clear that the advice being received from leading producers in Canada reflects very strongly the fact that they are not controlled from within Canada and hence not prepared to contemplate rationalizing in ways which might be possible if they were indigenous firms. The hostile reception which the National Advisory Committee on Petroleum gave to questions about the desirability of creating a large, vertically integrated Canadian controlled petroleum firm, similarly seems to be attribu-

table to the fact that most of the firms are not Canadian controlled.
These kinds of illustrations in part reflect only the fact that these
various industry associations advising Government act first and
foremost from self-interest. This is not surprising nor would one
expect Canadian controlled firms to behave differently. The point
is that the substance of their advice reflects the fact that these firms
do not always have the same interests as a Canadian controlled firm.
The central decision makers at headquarters are subject to pressures
from several countries. They are also more remote from Canadian
Government influence and bound to reflect these facts in their
decisions.

To take another example, the very strong pressure brought to
bear in respect of proposals for changes in taxation of mining firms
reflected partly the international scope of the industry and the fact
that most of the firms in it were multinational enterprises. Thus
they were able to threaten with some credibility that they would
shift resources to other countries in the event that the tax burdens
put upon them were too great. To a substantial degree, this was
also true of the Canadian-based multinationals. Or to take a different kind of case, the likelihood of securing the support of the
telecommunications carriers in the Telesat project might have been
much more difficult had these firms been foreign controlled.

Thus, on issues of industrial and related aspects of economic
policy, the political inputs and environment are influenced by
foreign control and the structure of the multinational enterprise.
On other aspects of public policy more generally, however, the
impact of intensive foreign control is less in evidence. Certainly
foreign controlled firms seem not to intervene politically on issues
of social, cultural and foreign policy. Their political behaviour in
these issues is not noticeably different than the behaviour of
Canadian controlled firms.

Impact of Foreign Controlled Firms on Public Policy

The first point which must be noted, even if evident, is that
foreign controlled firms have not had a direct influence on the
structure of the Canadian political system or on the choice of
Canadian Governments. This view is entirely consistent with the
conclusion above that foreign controlled firms seem not to intervene actively in such matters.

There is limited evidence of public policy being altered due to
the intervention of foreign governments into Canadian affairs to
protect the investments of their nationals. Public policy in respect
of English language magazines was influenced by the capacity of

Time (and to a much lesser degree, Reader's Digest) to obtain the support of the United States Government. This is, however, virtually the only case of its kind. In this case, incidentally, Maclean-Hunter now claims that its willingness to speak freely in the early 1960's was influenced by the threat of foreign controlled firms to withdraw their advertising, if Maclean's spoke out against the continuation of Time on the Canadian scene.

In the Mercantile case, the pressures brought to bear by the U.S. Government on behalf of that bank did not result initially in any change of substance in public policy. As the issue has now been resolved, this represents a compromise solution in which the fact of the intervention of the U.S. Government was obviously a factor, but by no means the overwhelming one.

Foreign controlled firms can affect the content of Canadian public policy even without consciously aiming to do this. For instance, the Government recognizes that certain kinds of policy alternatives are more or less impracticable because of the structure of certain industries and the fact that the firms in it are not controlled in Canada. The choices confronting Canada in industrial policy obviously are limited by the size and importance of the foreign controlled sector in Canada. Current policy in respect of the automobile and the rubber tire industries are only two examples of this. Commercial and competition policy must similarly reckon with the high degree of foreign control. Even balance of payments and monetary policy are significantly influenced by this factor and the international openness to which they contribute so heavily.

The capacity of the Government to implement policy can also be affected by foreign control. For instance, in the case of the balance of payments crisis at the beginning of 1968, the efforts of the Government were made more difficult by the announcement that foreign controlled firms would be subject to the U.S. balance of payments programme. Similarly, one aim of the Government's foreig policy is to diversify Canada's external ties and this is frustrated by the close trade, technological and personal links which accompany heavy U.S. investment. The extra-territorial application of U.S. trade and anti-trust legislation also serves to impede aspects of Canadian policy in respect of foreign trade and, to a much lesser degree, rationalization of domestic industry.

The fact that foreign control can hamper the implementation of policy has been recognized by the Government in certain aims of policy. For instance, the Government seems to have been of the view that the foreign subsidiary would be less able (or willing) to respond to the moral suasion of the Government than the Canadian controlled firm. For instance, the fact that no new foreign controlle banks can be chartered in Canada reflects in part the belief that it might be more difficult to implement monetary policy with foreign controlled banks in Canada; or possibly that such banks would have a greater capacity to defy the Bank of Canada. Even where moral suasion is not at issue, the Government has occasionally taken the view that foreign control can matter, e.g. in its decision not to allow foreign controlled firms to hold broadcasting licences. The implication of this decision is that the objectives of the Broadcasting Act cannot be achieved solely by Canadian content regulations; that to achieve the fullest implementation of Parliament's objectives, control must reside in the hands of Canadian citizens. These kinds of considerations provide some non-economic reasons for designating a sector as a "key sector".

In summary, foreign control does not seem to have had a direct bearing upon the Canadian political system or on the choice of Canadian Governments. It has, however, had some influence both on the content and implementation of public policy. With regard to the content of public policy, there is one (or at best two) case of foreign government intervention to support the interests of its investment in Canada which has affected public policy. But industrial policy and related aspects of economic policy are nevertheless heavily influenced by extensive foreign control. The logic of the multinational enterprises imposes constraints upon Canada's choices in these areas, this spills over into commercial policy and this impact radiates outward to influence other aspects of economic policy.

IMPACT OF FOREIGN CONTROL ON THE FORMULATION AND CONDUCT OF CANADIAN FOREIGN POLICY AND RELATIONS

It must be recognized that the impact of foreign control on the formulation and conduct of foreign policy is not simply a result of the behaviour of individual foreign controlled firms. Certainly, there is little evidence that foreign controlled firms set out deliberately and consciously to influence the Government with respect to general foreign policy — for example, to adopt a policy reflecting the views of the company owners or in tune with the national goals of the firm's home country. Nevertheless, the impact of foreign controlled firms on aspects of foreign policy can still be quite substantial, because of the way they indirectly affect certain foreign economic policy objectives, and more generally, due to their influence on the Canadian culture.

Formulation of Foreign Policy

CULTURE AND FOREIGN POLICY FORMULATION

The formulation and conduct of Canadian foreign policy are dependent in the first instance on the way in which national identity and interests are perceived. This perception grows out of the cultural (i.e. encompassing political, economic and social) environment, which is conditioned by a variety of factors, including inter alia foreign influences. Amongst these influences, that of the United States dominates. The U.S. influence in Canada clearly consists of more than U.S. direct investment in Canada. Nonetheless, U.S. investment has been one influential factor in shaping the general environment within Canada — the environment within which national identity and interests have been perceived and articulated and, more particularly, in which foreign policy has been formulated.

For many years after World War II, policy formation in Canada occurred within the framework of close international cooperation between western states which had grown up during that war and the adjustment period immediately thereafter. During those years, in a domestic situation of generally rapid economic development, foreign direct investment was widely considered to be an important benefit. Moreover, at that time, the perception of a distinctive Canadian identity and interests was not so evident as it is today.

More recently, some questions have been raised about these attitudes and policies, questions arising in part out of concern with the volume and concentration of foreign direct investment and also to some extent out of a fresh way of perceiving and articulating the values and interests broadly common to the 22 million Canadians. The White Paper on Foreign Policy dealt with these developments by focusing on the desirability of diversifying Canada's external relationships. Indeed, in principle, Government policy is to strengthen Canadian external relationships with Europe, including the EEC, and the Pacific, including Japan — rather than to be content with a mainly continental approach.

As a practical matter, however, there was little observable change in the pattern of foreign direct investment through that part of the 1960's for which statistical data are available. U.S. investment accounted for 80 per cent of direct investment Left unimpeded, it seems likely that private investment is likely to continue to come heavily from the U.S. This in turn means that Canadian culture is likely to continue to be influenced heavily by the large amount of U.S. direct investment, which must inevitably have some influence on the formulation of Canada's general posture to the world.

FOREIGN CONTROL AND FOREIGN POLICY FORMULATION – POLITICAL

There is little to show that the foreign policy options actually considered by the Government have been limited directly by the degree of U.S. business control in this country. Canada, for example, maintained diplomatic relations with Cuba when other western hemisphere countries broke them. The Canadian decision not to negotiate until recently for recognition of China took into account a variety of factors among which U.S. investment in Canada played no noticeable part. Of course, the major differences between the U.S. and Canada in the past 10 or 15 years, e.g., Cuba, China, Vietnam, have not been consciously exploited, and the Canadian view has often, in fact, been supported within the U.S. by important groups.

It is not clear how the U.S. would react should Canada strike out on a radically different foreign policy line, e.g., recognize East Germany, North Korea or North Vietnam, or enter into a non-aggression treaty with the U.S.S.R. or China. But any reaction is not likely to be motivated in Washington primarily by the volume of U.S. direct investment in Canada, but by a number of other considerations, including "ideological" and security factors – though it might well result in a much tougher line on the various economic "special arrangements" entered into over the years with Canada, e.g., the Automotive Products Agreements, the balance of payments exemptions and the Defence Production Sharing Arrangements.

FOREIGN CONTROL AND FOREIGN POLICY FORMULATION – ECONOMIC

As for trade, Canadian policy since World War II has been hinged largely on the desirability of a gradual multilateral reduction of barriers to trade. This has, by and large been achieved through successive multilateral trade negotiations under the auspices of the GATT. Since the Kennedy Round, efforts have been proceeding in GATT for further negotiations. Although preparatory work is nearly complete, there has been a lack of will to move to the negotiating stage. This is for several reasons. One is the resurgence of protection-ism in the U.S. and elsewhere. A second is the tendency toward regionalization of the world into two or three large trading blocs. They also pose graphically the Canadian dilemma, as from both the broad foreign policy and the trade policy points of view, Canada has been endeavouring to avoid North American economic integration.

Foreign control seems to influence the formulation of trade policy in three ways. Firstly, because of the propensity for intra-affiliate trade to grow relative to arms length trade, it seems to influence trade patterns. In this case, it seems to re-enforce the already strong trend toward north-south trade. If foreign direct investment in Canada were more diversified, trade patterns would probably also be more diversified.

Secondly, foreign control has an influence on the freedom of subsidiaries to procure and to export. In the past, these restrictions seem not to have been recognized sufficiently in the formulation of trade strategy. For instance, it is understood that in preparing the Canadian position during the Kennedy Round, relatively little attention was given to the ownership of firms. The best access possible was negotiated to export markets, without a careful study of corporate restrictions on the subsidiaries to export.

Finally, of course, careful attention is given to the representations of domestic industry in formulating trade strategy. Many of the firms are subsidiaries. Their views are either based on the position of their parent — or are at least consistent with it. Thus, indirectly, Canadian strategy can be influenced by interests of the parent firms of the subsidiary. In this case, this again means a very heavy U.S. influence, a fact which may not be lost on our other trading partners.

POLICY ON TRADE WITH COMMUNIST COUNTRIES

As this has been considered at length in the section on Extra-territoriality, it need simply be repeated here that policy toward communist countries can be affected by the influence of U.S. legislation and regulations on Canadian subsidiaires of U.S. firms. The converse of this situation is that since Canada recognized the Peoples' Republic of China, representatives of that country have declared that they do not wish to do business with United States subsidiaries.

The impact of foreign business control on the conduct of Canadian foreign relations is both direct and indirect. Direct influence is felt generally in the handling by the Government of relations with other countries and, more specifically, in the implementation of foreign economic policy. The impact of foreign direct investment is also indirect through the image of Canada abroad and views that others have of this country in the light of the degree and concentration of foreign ownership of Canadian industry.

This image affects the position other countries adopt toward Canada in negotiations and accordingly the Canadian capacity to realize policy objectives.

Conduct of Foreign Relations — Economic

CONDUCT OF CANADIAN RELATIONS WITH THE UNITED STATES

The issue of interest is how foreign control influences the conduct of relations with the U.S. In a general sense it is obvious that foreign control increases the links and complicates what would in any event be the most complex of Canada's foreign relations.

In addition, foreign control has facilitated the various special arrangements, especially in respect of automobiles, defence, production sharing, oil and balance of payments. Each of these is examined briefly below.

The point in common, in each case, is that foreign control has prompted or facilitated the special arrangements. In turn, the arrangements have deepened Canada's economic integration with the U.S., narrowing Canada's economic and political options.

In general, the Automotive Products Agreement has brought imported economic benefits to Canada. However, the price appears to be a diminished capacity for the Canadian Government to influence further the behaviour of this industry.

The Government has been told by industry that if it wishes the industry in Canada to act in a certain way — e.g., to increase production and investment — it should announce directives. But at the same time, the industry is undoubtedly aware that the U.S. Government may have the power to veto such guidelines by putting pressure on parent firms. In other words, domestic control of the automobile sector has been weakened.

As the subsidiaries cannot be expected to protect Canada's interests, continued direct intervention by the Canadian Government will be necessary. Inevitably, this will mean an additional issue in Canada — U.S. relations.

It is difficult to see how this kind of problem can be avoided in an industry as important as the automotive, with the degree of foreign control that exists in that industry. While there may be little that can be done in the immediate future, the screening process proposal, if accepted, could be of assistance in this kind of situation (though not a panacea).

The Defence Production Sharing Arrangement was entered into following cancellation of the Avro Arrow. At that time the Canadian Government decided that while Canada might not be able to maintain an independent military equipment capacity, it wished to ensure that the Canadian industrial economy benefitted from defence contracts and that the Canadian balance of payments did not suffer from large purchases abroad of defence material. The Arrangement envisages a rough balance of expenditures between Canada and the U.S. In fact, Canada has had a positive balance on defence equipment account with the U.S. and has developed a highly specialized defence related industrial capacity.

At the same time, the degree of U.S. ownership and control has increased noticeably with U.S. interests buying into an increasingly rationalized industry. U.S. influence is exercised also through licensing and other arrangements.

The U.S. control of the Canadian defence industry has made it difficult to develop similar defence production arrangements with other countries, notably the French and Germans, either because licensing agreements between Canadian, and U.S. firms contain restrictions which prevent the Canadians from using the licensed technology or weapons in arrangements with third countries, or because the third countries believe this to be the case. One impact has thus been to bind Canada more closely into the North American economic and defence framework.

It seems possible that the corporate links between oil companies in Canada and those in the U.S. have facilitated the access of Canadian oil to the U.S. market, an access which has traditionally been on better terms than accorded even to other western hemisphere suppliers. These special arrangements bring Canada in more tightly to the U.S. economy. From the viewpoint of foreign relations, they are a complicating factor — an additional point of difficulty in relation to the U.S.

While the Interest Equalization Tax and the Federal Reserve Guidelines — two of the elements in the U.S. Balance of Payments Programme — are not in any direct way linked to foreign direct investment, the Department of Commerce Guidelines are directed explicitly at U.S. direct investment abroad. The concern that the Department of Commerce provisions would apply in Canada, due to the high level of U.S. direct investment in this country, re-enforced the need for Canadian exemptions. This has been yet another factor bringing Canada into an even closer relationship with the U.S.

Direct investment provides additional handles which the U.S. could use to put pressure on Canada in respect to unrelated issues At the same time, the weight of evidence suggests that there has been little overt tendency on the part of the U.S. to whipsaw, i.e. to use pressure in one area to gain advantage in another. On occasion there do appear to have been efforts of this kind, e.g. recently by a senior State Department official (rather unsuccessfully) over the oil and Automotive Products Agreement discussion. There have also been suggestions that several years ago the U.S. linked the Time/Reader's Digest case with the willingness to be forthcoming on the automotive talks.

CONDUCT OF RELATIONS WITH COUNTRIES OTHER THAN THE U.S. – ECONOMIC

The situation described in the previous subsections has not been lost on European countries or Japan. The degree of U.S. control of Canadian business, and the policy affinities which exist between the two countries have undoubtedly prejudiced the Canadian position in realtions with third countries, including our ability to achieve foreign and commercial policy objectives.

In many areas Canada is in effect assimilated to the U.S. during international discussions and negotiations – and is regarded as having the same problems (if any) or on the basis that the U.S. can speak for Canada and hence negotiators may as well deal with the real authority. In this way actual and distinct Canadian problems, aims or differences of view can be overlooked. Thus there was a tendency among Europeans and others to equate the Canadian and U.S. viewpoints during the pre-negotiating stage and negotiations proper in the Kennedy Round. More recently, in the context of EEC enlargement negotiations, there has been a tendency for members of the EEC to deny that Canada has separate interests which need be taken in account. As mentioned, in the area of cooperation in production of defence equipment, both France and Germany in exploratory discussions have indicated some reluctance about becoming involved with firms in Canada on a shared production basis due to the links or special arrangements with U.S. firms.

In the eyes of some communist or neutral countries, the heavy U.S. control of Canadian business may tend to make Canada appear a "servant of U.S. capitalism" and thus undermine Canada's credibility as an independent nation This in turn could perhaps frustrate Canadian objectives in specific areas of foreign policy.

The countries of western Europe and Japan have for historical and other reasons become accustomed to owning domestically the great bulk of their own enterprises. There seems little doubt that they find hard to understand the nature of the Canada-U.S. relationship and the fact that we have allowed such a considerable amount of U.S. business control. (It seems unlikely, for example, that the French would have allowed the Germans to obtain the degree of penetration that the U.S. has achieved in Canada.) They have tended to conclude that Canada is in fact already fully tied in with the U.S. Their understanding of, for example. the Automotive Pact provides confirmation, to them, of this conclusion.

Implications and Recommendations

In the light of whatever the Government ultimately decides with respect to industrial development policy, it would seem desirable to work for a trade policy that emphasizes Canadian strengths and searches for ways to develop them through new kinds of arrangements with Europe and Pacific countries.

It would also seem desirable to examine the method of handling relations with the U.S.; there may be merit in considering whether more of an arms length relationship would not be possible and more in the Canadian interest.

It does appear to emerge from the anlaysis that one impact of American purchase of Canadian business is to accelerate the movement of goods and services between firms in a way that reduces the influence of governments on these flows. Moreover, this kind of acceleration of continental integration is generally stepped up on terms which are not in any way planned by the Canadian Government.

At a time when emerging world trade blocs pose the risk that Canada may be left outside a large regional group (unless Canada enters a full continental arrangement with the U.S.) it would seem important to consider the significance of these developments for basic Canadian foreign policy options. If Canada wishes to continue to limit continentalism, it makes little sense to maintain no controls at all on the development of ownership links which accelerate the process. Even should there at some point be a decision in favour of continentalism, some Government control of company ownership seems desirable; for in the absence of such controls, in for instance a free trade area, the likelihood is that American firms will move rapidly to acquire Canadian firms then to rationalize on a north-south basis, with the result that virtually all centres of innovation would be in the U.S.

A screening process, if adopted, could provide a mechanism to help deal with the foregoing developments. Steps taken to encourage Canadian industry to develop and innovate indigenously on an efficient basis should make Canada more able to maintain and develop relations on its own with a variety of countries. This in turn would serve basic Canadian policy objectives.

OTHER ISSUES

Foreign Government Investment in Canada

Foreign government investment is not likely ever to become a major part of the Canadian economy, although it could conceivably become significant in one or two resource industries. Moreover, the Canadian Government may well have, at least in some instances, more leverage against investment from governments, as diplomatic entities, than against the head offices of most multinational enterprises.

Accordingly, it would not seem necessary to bar, in principle, investment in Canada by foreign governments but rather to treat it generally as any other investment.

Non-Western Foreign Investment in Canada

It does not seem necessary to treat investment from "non-western", developing, countries differently from "western" investments. Communist country investments would first be subject to the screening process, if adopted, then to a further set of criteria being worked out to apply to such countries, in view of the special nature of our relations with them at present.

5

HOW GOVERNMENTS HAVE RESPONDED TO FOREIGN DIRECT INVESTMENT

CANADIAN POLICY TOWARDS FOREIGN DIRECT INVESTMENT

Canada has always welcomed foreign direct investment. However, certain measures have been taken through the years which have had the effect, directly or indirectly, either of limiting direct investment in certain areas of the economy, or of determining its terms of entry.

Heavy public investment in certain parts of the transportation, communications, atomic energy and hydro-electric industries ensured that there would always be an important Canadian presence in those parts of the economy. For instance, federal ownership of Canadian National, Air Canada and the Canadian Broadcasting Corporation has had the effect of limiting the scope for substantial non-resident control in those sectors. Similarly, provincial ownership of hydro-electric utilities and of some telephone companies has reduced the possibilities for foreign direct investment in those areas.

A second way in which foreign investment has been partially controlled has been through public regulation of certain parts of the economy. Such public regulation was not, of course, directed particularly at foreign controlled firms. Nevertheless, it had the effect of helping to ensure that the foreign controlled firms behaved in a way consistent with Canadian policy objectives, e.g. in transportation, energy.

Public policy has responded in three other ways — through certain restrictions on foreign investment, through measures to increase the benefits and reduce the costs of foreign investment and through efforts to encourage Canadian ownership.

The response of various Federal and Provincial Governments to extensive foreign direct investment in Canada has largely been piecemeal.

Certain measures have been implemented which, while by no means directed specifically at foreign subsidiaries, have had the impact of ensuring a large Canadian presence in those industries.

Secondly, restrictions on foreign control, to one degree or other, have been introduced in certain key sectors of the economy. These have been applied largely in response to fears of foreign takeovers.

Thirdly, various efforts have been made to improve the performance of foreign controlled firms in Canada. On the whole, these have not been very effective.

Finally, some efforts have been made to stimulate Canadian ownership, but these have thus far not apparently had any substantial impact on the pattern of foreign ownership in the economy.

POLICIES OF OTHER GOVERNMENTS TOWARD FOREIGN DIRECT INVESTMENT

Introduction: Purpose and Method

This section describes how other governments have responded to inward foreign direct investment. It does not consider their policies on imports of portfolio investment. The purpose of the section is simply to provide some idea of the range of policies which prevail abroad and the instruments used to implement them.

The sources of information include special reports prepared by Canadian missions abroad as well as the published literature. The countries examined included eleven advanced, or relatively advanced, industrial countries of Western Europe, the United States, Australia, South Africa, Japan and Mexico. Although Italy and South Africa are in some respects less fully developed than the remaining countries, Mexico is the only one not normally considered to be a developed country.

There are four considerations which must be taken into account in assessing the findings below.

The first is that, in relation to the size of their domestic economies, none of the countries are experiencing a degree of foreign control which remotely resembles the Canadian situation. The reasons for this vary from case to case. At least two of the countries have devised policies particularly because of a fear of extensive foreign control by a nearby neighbour (Norway and Mexico).

On the other hand, a number of countries are experiencing a high degree of foreign control in select high technology industries and certain other capital intensive activities. The German petrochemical industry, for instance, and the British automobile industry, are largely controlled from abroad. But, on the whole no other country has a situation remotely resembling the Canadian picture.

Secondly, most of the countries surveyed adhere to the OECD Code for the Liberalization of Capital Movements. As they have accepted, in principle, the desirability of freeing capital movements, they normally tend to emphasize the more liberal aspects of their policies. Incidentally, while Canada is more liberal than most other countries, Canada alone amongst the OECD countries does not adhere to this Code.

Thirdly, these countries include the world's largest exporters of capital, including the United States, the United Kingdom, Germany, Switzerland, Sweden and the Netherlands. As such, they have important vested interests in striving for relative ease of access for the intended overseas investments of their nationals and for ease of repatriation of profits. To varying degrees, this fact serves as a liberalizing pressure on their policies towards capital imports. It seems also to lead them to take a relatively relaxed attitude about the practices of multinational enterprises.

Finally, all countries studied, except the U.S. and Switzerland, have in place a foreign exchange control apparatus. Some use it restrictively; others are more liberal. Exchange controls were not implemented in these countries with the primary aim of preserving domestic ownership and control of the economy (except possibly in Japan), but rather for balance of payments reasons. As balance of payments considerations have permitted, most countries have generally tended to rely progressively less on the exchange control mechanism in dealing with current payments. However, as an outgrowth of their earlier balance of payments problems, most countries do have the experience of an exchange control apparatus capable of regulating capital imports.

Each of the countries studied has its own historical experience and special peculiarities. Accordingly, each policy is unique. However, for summary purposes, certain arbitrary lines can be drawn to provide an overview of other countries' policies.

It will be noted that some countries are discussed under more than one of the policy headings below as elements of their practice make it difficult to put the country under any single one. The headings are:

a. liberal or very liberal;
b. countries wishing to attract foreign investment but which bargain about its terms and conditions of entry;
c. countries seeking to perfect key sectors;
d. nationalistic or restrictive.

Policy Approaches

I. VERY LIBERAL OR LIBERAL

Countries which have very few restrictions on direct foreign investment include the United States, Netherlands, West Germany and Denmark. It should be noted that the first three of these countries are important capital exporters or have major investments abroad. The U.S. is, of course, the largest capital exporter and bastion of the multinational enterprise and as such has an interest in freer movements of capital.

The West German economy is also based upon liberal economic principles. In the past, the West Germans seem to have been prepared to welcome U.S. investments in Germany, partly with a view to increasing the American commitment to the protection of West Berlin and of Germany against aggression by the Soviet Union.

The Netherlands is both very anxious to attract foreign capital for economic and regional development purposes, and to protect the enormous investments of its giants, e.g. Shell, Unilever and Phillips (which are partially controlled in the Netherlands). Denmark is also anxious to attract foreign capital for economic development purposes.

At the same time, through one device or another, even these countries have from time to time made it difficult for foreigners to invest in particular industries.

COUNTRIES WISHING TO ATTRACT INVESTMENT BUT WHICH BARGAIN ABOUT TERMS AND CONDITIONS

Some countries within this classification are relatively liberal; others are much less so. The main point here is that each uses the apparatus available to it to negotiate to meet the needs of its own economy. The U.K. (a major exporter of capital) formally prohibits all investments until the conditions it sets are met, and this involves discussions between the U.K. authorities and the investors about a variety of factors in the more important cases. Similarly the Australians, Belgians and Italians seek to attract foreign investments but bargain to maximize the contribution which the investment will make to their particular needs, e.g. bargaining for commitments for export performance and for location in a designated area.

France's policy has varied through the last ten years, but has normally been rather more nationalistic than the above countries. However, France also bargains about the terms and conditions of foreign entry. Norway's position is quite similar to that of the French. The principle, in each case, is that while the foreigner has something of value to the host economy, the host also has an asset the foreigner wants — easy access to its domestic markets.

C.   COUNTRIES SEEKING TO PROTECT KEY SECTORS

Some of the countries listed below have been or will be referred to under other categories also. The principal countries here are Sweden and Norway, both of which claim to be very liberal, but which in fact exclude or restrict foreign investment across wide and important parts of their economy, especially in resources. In addition, Italy, Austria, France and the U.S. have fairly significant parts of their economy which are not open to the foreign investor, or in which the foreigner can obtain only restricted access.

In contrast, the United Kingdom, Denmark, Belgium, West Germany and Switzerland rely very little on this kind of approach. The selection of key sectors, where this is an important policy element, seems to be based on a few clearly defined criteria and the considerations apparently vary widely from one country to the other. Sectors most frequently designated include banking, insurance, parts of communications and transportation, including public utilities and natural resources.

D.   NATIONALIST OR RESTRICTIVE

The prime examples of a nationalistic policy are Mexico and Japan, both of which have had a very different historical and cultural experience from the other countries considered here. In Mexico, where there was substantial foreign ownership prior to the 1910 revolution, foreign capital is used only as a supplement to internal savings.

In Japan, where the foreigner has traditionally been suspect, every effort has been made to hold out foreign participation for as long as possible, while domestic industry readied itself to compete on an international basis.

In both cases, the degree of foreign investment is very small. It must be further noted that, in the case of France, Sweden and Norway, there are important nationalistic overtones and a strong desire to ensure that ownership of a fairly wide sector of the economy remains in the hands of the nationals. In all cases, it is apparent that the reasoning is largely due to politico-strategic and/or cultural reasons and relate rather less to overall economic performance. At the same time, one would be hard pressed to demonstrate conclusively that these economies suffered as a consequence. Indeed, there appears to be little correlation between national economic performance and the degree of a country's liberalism or restrictionism in respect of direct investment inflows.

Policy Elements

There are aspects of the experiences of other countries which are being examined in the Canadian review of policy and which therefore merit further comment here.

A GENERAL SCREENING PROVISION WHEREBY ALL FOREIGN INVESTMENT REQUIRES GOVERNMENT APPROVAL

A screening process is used systematically in Norway, France, Japan, Mexico and the United Kingdom, and to a lesser extent in Italy, Belgium, Sweden, Denmark, Austria and Australia. In most instances, a foreign exchange control apparatus exists with which to back up statutory requirements about notifications of foreign investment.

In some cases, the screening mechanism serves to prevent foreigners from making direct investments in particular industries; that is, permission is not granted. In Norway and Sweden, for instance, it would appear that it is virtually impossible for a foreigner to gain control of wooded lands or paper mills, even though these apparently are not, in any formal sense, key sectors. In Italy, investments may be turned down, if the foreigner wishes to invest in an industry in which state ownership is extensive. In other countries, the need to obtain governmental approval enables the recipient country to bargain about local equity participation, export undertakings, the presence of nationals on the board of directors, location of plant, procurement of services, or whatever considerations the recipient country judges relevant.

For instance, in Japan screening begins with the Bank of Japan, which has control of the exchange control apparatus. The Bank requires relevant information from would-be foreign investors. It then passes the information to the various concerned ministries, which in turn meet at a senior interdepartmental level. They may ask for changes in the investment and these are negotiated before the Minister of Finance will approve.

A similar process is followed in France but with greater emphasis on bargaining and less on rejecting investments. In France, this extends to screening of licensing agreements (e.g. on technology) to ensure that the terms are reasonable.

In the U.K., it is also usual to seek performance undertakings in cases of major takeovers. For instance, in the 1967 acquisitions of Rootes by Chrysler and of Pye by Phillips, undertakings were obtained to maintain or to increase exports.

DOMESTIC BORROWING RESTRICTIONS

Many countries have requirements respecting non-resident direct investment whereby all or a part of it must be financed from abroad. Such policies are normally justified on balance of payments grounds. In some cases this applies to all investments; in other cases it may apply only to takeovers. The access of non-resident controlled companies to domestic money markets, for working capital or for capital for investments in new fixed assets, may also be subject to limitation.

In the U.K. takeovers are expected to be entirely financed from abroad, and new enterprises to be financed largely from abroad. Foreign controlled firms are not normally expected to borrow domestically once the business is operating. In France, takeovers by non-resident firms of French companies must be entirely financed from abroad; for new enterprises, at least 50 per cent of the financing must be non-French.

In Italy investments are divided between "productive" and "non-productive". Foreign investments which do not involve creation or expansion of production facilities, for instance, the purchase of existing shares (a share swap or other form of takeover), is normally deemed to be "unproductive". The unproductive investments are discouraged by limiting free transferability abroad of interest, dividends and profits; and by limiting re-transfer abroad of the original investment resulting from disinvestment to an amount not exceeding the amount of foreign currency originally imported. It appears also that "productive" investments are freer to raise capital on the Italian capital markets than are "non-productive" investments.

In Australia, local borrowing by firms is affected by the extent of Australian equity participation in the economy, and in Norway the acceptance of a foreign investment is also affected by the amount of capital imported. There also seem to be similar provisions in South Africa, Mexico and Japan.

In all cases the aims seem to include one or more of the following: to strengthen the balance of payments; to use this as an indirect means of discouraging foreign investment, or of chanelling it into those industries where the host government wishes it; to encourage foreign firms to provide for equity participation by the nationals of the host country; and possibly to prevent displacement of local borrowers.

Other Techniques for Restricting Foreign Investment

Several countries have in their companies' legislation provisions which bear on foreign investment. Swedish firms have the right to limit, through their articles of association, the right of non-Swedish nationals to acquire shares in the company. In these cases, non-Swedes are normally restricted to a 20 per cent interest in aggregate. In practice, 39 of the 40 largest Swedish companies have made use of this provision and thus effectively prevented foreigners from acquiring control.

In Switzerland, corporations can issue their common shares in three forms, "Participation shares" enable a shareholder to participate equally in profits with other common shareholders but not to vote; "registered" common shares are available only to Swiss citizens; "bearer" common shares may be held by citizens of any country. The latter two types have voting rights. Registered shares are always in the majority and thus this precludes foreign acquisition.

Japan also requires that companies have different categories of shares and foreigners are permitted to purchase only a designated category.

Restrictions on the purchase or lease of real property by non-nationals in Norway, Denmark, Sweden and Switzerland enable the authorities in those countries to use this as a tool for bargaining or for restricting foreign investment.

Takeovers

In general, national governments tend to distinguish between takeovers by foreigners and the starting up of new enterprises by foreigners. Even some of the more liberal countries, such as West Germany, Australia and Belgium, have prevented takeovers through ad hoc administrative practices. The Belgium Government is now introducing a new law respecting foreign takeovers. In Italy, as already indicated, a takeover is normally deemed to be "non-productive" unless the enterprise purchased is to be expanded by the acquiring firm. Such non-productive investment is likely to be discouraged through restrictions on the access of such firms to the domestic money markets for loans, and through limitations on repatriation both of profits, interest, other current payments and of the capital investment itself.

France requires that foreign takeovers be financed entirely through foreign currency. In addition, it has used its screening authority to discourage takeovers.

In Switzerland, requirements for nationals on the boards of directors, limitations on work permits and land permits, and the technique of using different categories of shares, referred to above, all make takeovers very difficult.

The constrained share status of almost all leading Swedish companies is an important barrier to the takeover of Swedish firms. Takeovers of Japanese firms are unheard of. In Australia there is a takeover code and the Government will intervene to prevent takeovers when the national interest requires it.

The general philosophy which underpins each of these countries' policies includes one or more of the following: straight nationalistic opposition to foreigners; desire of domestic corporate management to fend off foreign takeovers; government wish to channel foreign investment into areas where it will be most productive, which means into new investments rather than acquisitions; allowance of takeovers only after negotiations on performance have been successful.

Key Sectors

Because of widespread restrictions on foreign investment in Mexico and Japan, the key sector analysis cannot be readily applied to those two countries. However, now that Japan claims to be liberalizing, she has established two lists of industries in which investment will be severely restricted, even in the long-run. One negative list includes banking, electricity, gas and water utilities, railways and other transportation utilities, maritime and air transport, mining, broadcasting, fishing, port and harbour operations and trustee business. The other deals with modern technologically-oriented industries and automobiles.

Sweden and Norway restrict foreign control in real property, waterfalls, minerals, forest resources and shipping. Denmark restricts foreign participation in financial institutions and farming. The French are most concerned about electronics, information software and automobiles, and West Germany oil refining, automobiles and electronics. The Italians protect banking, insurance, finance, shipping and air transportation; the Australians banking and broadcasting. In the U.S. foreign participation is prohibited or restricted in shipping, broadcasting, communication satellites, hydro-electric power, or activities associated with atomic energy and banks. In addition, some countries have "catch-all" phrases relating to strategic industries. Moreover many other industries are restricted from foreigners implicitly through the fact of state monopolies.

The reasons why other governments designate key sectors is seldom made clear. In some cases it clearly reflects historical concern about what were, in the past, industries of great strategic importance, either for military or economic reasons. Thus, most countries ensure that key financial institutions, communications and transportation facilities are under the control of their citizens.

The other general reason seems to reflect a concern about the high technology, high growth industries which may dominate the future. Governments apparently believe that a strong indigenous capacity is important for their national interests.

MANDATORY HOST COUNTRY SHAREHOLDINGS

The issue of mandatory local shareholdings clearly does not arise in Japan or Mexico, where the law requires that local shareholders always (or almost always) retain control.

In general, most governments, except the most liberal, tend to look more kindly upon foreign investments in which opportunity is provided for domestic equity ownership on a partnership basis.

Thus the French or Italians will be more likely to approve a 51:49 or 50:50 venture than one in which there is no intended domestic participation. Even where investments are permitted, access to local borrowing may not be allowed in the absence of large local shareholdings.

On the other hand, it appears that only Australia attaches importance to local portfolio shareholdings in foreign controlled firms. The degree to which these portfolio holdings are permitted determines whether foreign controlled firms may borrow money in Australia.

Board of Directors

Many countries require a majority of nationals on boards of directors. They include the three Scandinavian countries which are examined here. The Australian Government emphasizes the importance it attaches to having Australian nationals on boards of directors and in senior management. It does not require this by law but creates some pressures to obtain such representation. Where foreigners are entitled to up to 50 per cent of a Japanese company, management remains entirely Japanese, and the percentage of Japanese equity must carry with it an equal number of Japanese directors.

The British also prefer to see a majority of their nationals on boards of directors and while information is not available on some of the other countries, the availability of a bargaining tool has probably led some of them to also impose such requirements.

Conclusion

Some countries have clearly articulated policies; others have proceeded on a case by case basis. This illustrates the wide range of possibilities within the western liberal economic system and the variety of instruments available for the implementation of government objectives.

Generally, most countries seem to have a sense of national interest, however muddled and inarticulate it may be. What it seem to say is that business enterprise is most easily made to serve the national interest if owned and run by nationals. The norm is to hav domestic ownership and control. Under pressure to liberalize, both from capital exporting countries (especially the United States) and from the important economies of scale in certain industries (e.g. aerospace, computer hardware), national governments have been prepared to countenance some increase in non-national contre of national business.

While there is thus a tendency towards liberalization, the pace is slow and uneven. Nor is the liberal trend necessarily a continuou process. Even in the most liberal countries it seems likely that, if there were widespread foreign control, a halt would be called. This may be reading too much into other countries' policies, but, from isolated measures of the more liberal countries, it seems a justified conclusion.

Perhaps the single most common policy instrument of other countries is the use of some form or other of screening mechanism. It can be used to restrict or to bargain, or both. It provides flexibility from time to time and case to case.

6

CONCLUSIONS
AND IMPLICATIONS
OF BASIC ANALYSIS

CONCLUSIONS

The conclusions which are highlighted below by no means reflect all of the Findings and Analysis contained in the prevous four sections. However, they do point to the main findings and these are dealt with in the three sub-sections below.

Domestic Control of the National Economic Environment

The Findings and Analysis suggest that foreign control of domestic business affects adversely domestic control of the national economic environment. This is due mainly to the fact of foreign control per se and, secondarily, to the fact that the operations of these firms are international in scope.

Domestic control of the national economic environment is reduced by the limitations which foreign direct investment imposes on our choices in industrial policy, particularly with respect to the kinds of rationalization that are feasible, e.g. industrial chemicals, oil. Thus, certain alternatives are not open to Canada simply because an industry or firm which is foreign controlled or international in scope cannot logically agree to certain forms of rationalization.

The Findings and Analysis have also suggested that the Government's capacity to implement policy can be hampered by the fact that a firm is foreign controlled, e.g. efforts to diversify trade and technological ties are impeded by foreign control.

Finally, Canadian law can be more readily frustrated by firms whose operations are international in scope (particularly those which are foreign controlled). Transfer prices for goods and services can be used to shift profits from one country to another and reduce tax revenues. Competition policy can also be frustrated.

Maximizing the Benefits and Minimizing the Costs of Foreign Direct Investment

The Findings and Analysis suggest that current policies are not geared closely enough to maximizing the benefits and minimizing the costs of foreign direct investment. With respect to economic benefits and costs, it was noted that competition policy is important in transmitting the economic benefits of foreign investment to the market place. The revisions which Cabinet has approved, in principle, to the Combines Investigations Act, should result in some improvements. Direct Government intervention in particular industries has strengthened the net benefits to Canada from foreign direct investment (mainly thus far in automobiles) but there is no general industrial strategy now in place which would help maximize the benefits to Canada from foreign investment.

As regards the non-economic costs and benefits, some efforts have been made to mitigate the adverse influence of the U.S. Trading with the Enemy Act and the extra-territorial application of the U.S. anti-trust law. These have not successfully met all the political objections to these problems, however, and no solution has yet been found to other manifestations of U.S. extra-territoriality.

With respect to foreign control of areas of cultural activity (e.g. broadcasting), some measures have been taken, but there has been no policy response to the more general cultural impact of direct investment on manufacturing and resources.

Increasing Canadian Ownership

The Findings and Analysis drew attention to the following factors affecting the possibility of increased Canadian ownership.

1. Foreign ownership and control is continuing to increase both in absolute and relative terms, though in relative terms the rate of increase was slower in the 1960's than in the 1950's.

2. The natural resource requirements of Japan and United States are likely to result in continued large investment from these countries for Canadian natural resources during the 1970's, suggesting the possibility of further increases in foreign control, at least in the resource sector.

3. The relative lack of "distinctiveness" in Canadian output, and the continued receptiveness of the Canadian economy to foreign distinctiveness, will likely continue to result in large sales of U.S. products in Canada. With the tariff, there is a

propensity to achieve these sales through investment rather than trade. This should ensure continued high (and possibly higher) degrees of foreign control in manufacturing.

4. The past high degree of foreign control has helped to perpetuate gaps in Canadian capital markets, technology, management etc. and, more generally, in entrepreneurship. This does not augur well for increasing Canadian control and ownership.

5. Neither the present tax law, nor the changes proposed in the White Paper on Tax Reform, even in conjunction with the CDC, are likely in themselves to change these trends.

In summary, it is being suggested that the above Findings and Analysis indicate that the objectives noted at the outside for Government policy are not being met to a satisfactory degree by the current mix of Government policies.

IMPLICATIONS

In the light of these conclusions and the Findings and Analysis above, there are a number of major *implications* for public policy.

a. While Canadian control of a business is important in some situations, it is not, in itself, a viable proxy for good corporate behaviour or domestic control. Hence a policy based on ownership alone is inappropriate;

b. There is a need for direct intervention by the Government in respect of foreign direct investment, as general economic policies cannot alone satisfy Government objectives;

c. There is justification for intervening only in respect of foreign controlled firms;

d. Such intervention ought to be flexible by industry and over time;

e. In addition to direct intervention, there is a parallel need for revising some general economic policies, to improve the benefits from foreign direct investment, e.g. competition, technology, capital markets, tariff, etc.

f. Foreign direct investment integrates Canada into the world economy. This integration can take various forms, which can generally be divided into two categories: branch plant truncation or branch plant rationalization.

g. Canadian subsidiaries are generally marginal operations in the sense that they are part of a broader organization and seldom have the capacity to survive independently of the links to their foreign parents.

h. Foreign direct investment, and in particular the multinational enterprise, involves a replacement of the international market place by decisions of international firms as a technique for allocating world resources. Public policies based on the assumption of a free international market are thus not likely to have as effective an impact on international trade and other forms of exchange as they would have in the past;

i. The non-economic impact of foreign direct investment may require special rules in a few selected industries and modifications in aspects of external policy.

The Relevance of Canadian Control for Corporate Behaviour and Domestic Control of the Economy

The Findings and Analysis have indicated to us a two-fold theme with respect to the relevance of Canadian ownership and control. First, the evidence does *not* indicate substantially better Canadian performance by Canadian controlled firms than by foreign controlled firms with respect to expenditures on research and development, exports and further processing.

The analysis also suggested certain other conclusions with respect to the importance of Canadian controlled firms. One was that they alone are able to have complete mastery of their business strategy and freedom to buy and sell according to their own interests. Foreign controlled firms, particularly multinational enterprises, are constrained by the interests of the parent and the strategy which it follows in achieving its goals.

The analysis suggested also that foreign controlled firms are subjected to a wider range of pressures than Canadian controlled firms. Accordingly, it is more difficult for the Government of Canada to influence the behaviour of foreign controlled firms than it is to influence that of Canadian controlled firms. And among Canadian controlled firms, it is more difficult to influence the behaviour of the Canadian multinational enterprises than it is to influence that of the largely domestically oriented Canadian controlled firms.

These two conclusions are important. First, they indicate that striving for Canadian control will not in itself be a guarantee of superior performance. In particular, it suggests that a policy based upon Canadian control alone (e.g. a 51 per cent rule) would be no guarantee of satisfactory corporate behaviour, and at the same time would give rise to other serious problems.

At the same time, it has been equally apparent that a policy which pays no attention to Canadian ownership is inappropriate.

Canadian control may be important in activities where the Government relies heavily on moral suasion to obtain a result (e.g. banking). It may also be important where non-economic objectives are at issue (e.g. broadcasting).

Equally important, a policy which pays no attention to Canadian control could result in Canadian secondary industry being nothing more than a satellite economy, entirely dependent upon foreign investment. If that were to happen, Canada would be virtually stripped of all capacity to develop indigenous technology, and the other forms of indigenous distinctiveness, which would enable it to specialize and penetrate domestic and world markets without corporate restriction. Certainly, the largest part of the benefits of the technologies and products developed abroad will almost always naturally be retained for the home economy.

In the future, it is likely that a Canadian industrial strategy will help select those lines of production in which Canada will specialize. If that happens, it is probable that heavy public expenditures and much labour will be concentrated in those lines. In that event, it would be unwise to leave open the possibility that decisions affecting the markets and technology of such a firm could be taken abroad by a foreign parent as part of the global strategy of a foreign firm. That is, Canadian control is very important in such cases.

In future areas of Canadian specialization, particularly where economies of scale require it, Canadian based multinational enterprises may emerge. When this happens, especially if the U.S. market becomes dominant, there is the danger that these firms will be uprooted from their Canadian origins and acquire, through time, U.S. citizenship, in reality if not in name. Where Canadian policy does foster Canadian control and Canadian based multinational enterprises, Government policy will have to take into account the need for devising techniques for rooting these firms in Canada.

There is Need for Direct Intervention by the Government

The first major implication of the Findings and Analysis is that there is a need for direct intervention by the Government in respect of inflows of foreign direct investment.

The openness of the Canadian economy can result in Canadian industrial priorities being distorted by foreign direct investment. This is because foreign investors tend to be more heavily influenced by the environment and priorities of other countries rather than of Canada. Foreign direct investment brings with it a pool of costs and benefits; there is some scope for altering the net benefits obtainable by Canada from direct Government intervention. The scope for bargaining is re-enforced by the analysis above where it was suggested that the distinctiveness of the investor and the fact of sunk costs, can result in a profit level sufficiently attractive to the investor that there is room for bargaining.

Canadian ownership objectives can be assisted by a policy which encourages, where economically efficient, joint ventures or the seeking out of alternative Canadian owners. Canadian controlled firms, and the Canadian economy, would benefit from the capacity of the Government to screen the terms and conditions of licensing agreements, especially arms length agreements.

These domestic economic policies will not, however, get at the imperfections of the international market place in allocating industrial activity, nor will they themselves overcome any institutional biases of the multinational enterprise of the foreign investor. They will not deal with the phenomenon of market power, which is rooted outside of Canada, nor easily offset the interventions of other governments in influencing the location and trade decisions of the multinational enterprise. Furthermore, general rules, by their nature, do not cover most effectively situations which differ greatly. As a result, important objectives of a screening process could not be realized through such policies.

Some objectives of direct intervention through a screening process are:

1. The protection of industrial priorities
2. Bargaining for a better deal
3. Blocking of foreign investment which adds nothing of value
4. Bargaining with foreign proprietors of technology or other valuable inputs for arms length transfer to Canada
5. Selectively protect Canadian entrepreneurship

If the general economic policies perform well, fewer problems will arise and foreign controlled industry — like all industry — will operate with greater efficiency. Without intervention, however, undesirable foreign investment will not necessarily be resisted, and Canadian control will not necessarily be substituted for foreign control where that is economically feasible. The terms of foreign investment will generally improve, but may not be maximized for each unique setting, at different points in time and in view of new distinctive capacities in Canada or elsewhere. To achieve some of these results through techniques other than a screening process, domestic policies may become excessively distorted.

The various techniques considered above frequently engender retaliatory steps by other governments seeking to retain their levels of activity. Intergovernmental rivalry of this sort could be costly and

Canada might find itself at a decided disadvantage — particularly in competition with the U.S. A screening process might attract less retaliation.

Justification for Intervening only in Respect of Foreign Controlled Firms

While many of the reasons for intervention apply also to Canadian controlled firms, four factors justify some discrimination against foreign controlled firms.

The first reason is that the benefits of Canadian controlled investment are enjoyed exclusively by Canadians. If the distribution of the benefits within Canadian society is judged to be unsatisfactory, it is for domestic, economic and social policy to rectify this. In the case of foreign investment, a portion of the benefits are siphoned out of the country. Thus, it is a legitimate aim of public policy to intervene so as to maximize the benefits which remain in Canada.

Secondly, Canadian controlled firms are not as heavily influenced by the foreign environment and foreign governments as are foreign controlled firms. They are more likely to be sensitive to the local environment and the demands of the local economy.

Thirdly, foreign controlled firms, and in particular the multi-national enterprise have a greater capacity to frustrate Canadian policy than do Canadian controlled firms.

Finally, some of the non-economic costs are not incurred as a result of domestic investment. In particular, the problems of the extra-territorial application of foreign law, as well as the political and cultural problems raised above, do not arise.

Thus, it is possible to justify a policy which involves intervention in respect of foreign direct investment.

Intervention Ought to be Flexible

The third main implication of the Findings and Analysis is that direct intervention by the Government ought not to be based on any rigid pre-determined set of rules but rather upon a more flexible approach. It is important that rigid rules do not cut Canada off from new developments abroad which are not available in forms other than direct investment. More generally, foreign direct investment involves both costs and benefits, and the distribution of costs and benefits will vary from one situation to the other. While it may ultimately be possible to develop specific rules pertaining to industries, it is evident that flexibility from one industry to another, and from one point in time to another, is essential. In this connection, foreign direct investment sometimes does add incremental economic activity in Canada and at other times it does not.

Need to Revise General Economic Policies

The Findings and Analysis also make clear that general economi policies (e.g., competition, technology, tax, tariff, capital markets) are matters which influence the costs and benefits derived from foreign investment and, by their impact on economic efficiency, o the benefits which Canada obtains.

The foreign manufacturer enters Canada either because he sees a larger profit in investing here than he does through trade; or he ma invest in Canada to preclude the possibility that a Canadian or a foreign competitor will locate in Canada. One factor which has in the past served to draw him to Canada has been the level of the tariff. The rate of protection it provided, which, as explained above may exceed the nominal tariff level, provided a cushion for inefficiency or added profit. While the tariff is probably a smaller consideration today, it remains as one factor. The absence of a vigorou anti-combines policy re-enforces the incentive to locate here by allowing for higher profits and tends to lead to the branch plant miniature replica effect. Thus, while there are employment benefit at least in the short run, obtained from the foreign direct investment attracted by these general economic policies, they encourage an industrial structure which produces a wide range of products at substantially less than optimal efficiency. This means higher cos and hence higher prices to consumers. It means also that Canadian manufacturers are not required by market pressures to specialize and hence their costs are such that they cannot readily penetrate world markets.

A more vigorous anti-combines policy and a significantly lower level of tariff protection would likely increase the benefits to Canada from foreign direct investment. A less restrictive patent policy should have the same effect.

The Marginal Nature of the Subsidiary

Most subsidiaries are not capable of operating independently of the parent. They rely upon parental inputs, lack skills, are devoid any distinctiveness and are thus locked into a technological and overhead pattern (based on product differentiation and development, etc.) which would not allow the subsidiary to operate independently of the global unit.

This last point means that in addition to being truncated, Canadian subsidiaries are frequently *marginal* operations, in the sense that they are part of a broader organization and operate in a fashion which can only be supported on the basis of marginal economics tied into a larger firm. The technology used would often be inappropriate to the subsidiary, except as part of the international firm. The product line and marketing style tend to depend on the broader corporate operations. The Canadian subsidiary on its own would experience higher costs per unit, if it attempted to continue its former style of operations. The change-over of technology might be prohibitive.

This in turn has an important bearing on those who advocate "buy back" as a central theme of policy. In the case of manufacturing subsidiaries at least, this is generally not viable because the body is not of much use without the brain; and the brain is abroad. The subsidiary — the body — may be worth a lot to the parent which controls it. Left on its own it would wither.

Foreign Direct Investment and the Multinational Enterprise Reduce the Role of the International Market

The evidence showed that a large and growing proportion of international trade is between affiliated firms. It showed also that most of the trade of firms which have international affiliates is between the affiliates — not on an arms length basis.

The implications of these facts are several fold: one is that the distribution of production between different countries is not based on market forces, and consequently constitutes a reason for intervening. This was referred to above. Another is that trade and industrial development policy must come to grips with the above factor. In particular, proportionately more attention probably has to be given to negotiating with firms about their capacity and readiness to penetrate foreign markets. Our trade strategy must recognize that much of Canada's international commerce does not rest exclusively or primarily on tariff and Governmental non-tariff barriers to trade but on other factors, including corporate decisions.

Trade Can be a Substitute for Investment

Any policy which focuses on Canadian ownership and control, either as an end in itself, or as a proxy for good economic behaviour, must take account of the fact that trade may flow in the absence of investment.

For instance, if foreign investment is blocked, for whatever reason, the foreigner may be able to export here instead. Accordingly, the purpose of any Government policy affecting investment flows must be clear. If it is not, then it will not be evident what kind of tariff ought to accompany the action on investment.

The relationship between trade and investment patterns raises the question of the significance of the evolving trading blocs for the pattern of foreign investment in Canada. If a continental trading community were to develop between Canada and the U.S. larger markets would become available for Canadian firms. However, the removal of the cost advantage of local production in Canada which the tariff barrier provides would tend to reduce the incentives for U.S. firms to invest in Canada. In many cases, U.S. investment would thus not be replaced by domestic investment but by trade.

Indeed, one likely scenario, in the event of the creation of a North American free trade area, is that the typically larger U.S. firms would adjust first. To gain quick access to Canadian marketing channels, they would acquire existing Canadian firms. Subsequently, they would rationalize production between their U.S. and Canadian plants. In doing so, they would almost assuredly centre all the innovative and creative activities at U.S. headquarters.

"Gaps" in the domestic environment also make Canada a less convenient place for the location of further investment. In the absence of some intervention to rectify these conditions, this will continue as a further factor which would adversely influence the distribution of investment to the disadvantage of Canada. The high degree of foreign control and the existing deficiencies in Canadian capacities thus reduce the capacity of Canada to enter a continental relationship from a position of sufficient strength. Where a stronger, independent, Canadian controlled industry is achievable without serious economic cost, it is worthwhile pursuing if genuine continentalism is expected to come in the future. To the extent that continental integration is resisted, a stronger Canadian industrial base is equally important, even though the industries selected might not be the same.

The Need for Industrial Development Strategy

It has been pointed out above that there is a need for direct intervention in respect of foreign direct investment and for revisions to aspects of general economic policies. In themselves, these proposals could have an important influence on the benefits which Canada derives from foreign direct investment.

At the same time, it is clear that the benefits would be greatly enhanced if these changes could be implemented within a framework which made clear the ultimate purposes of these instruments. An industrial development strategy would provide such a framework.

Furthermore, it has been pointed out that foreign direct investment integrates Canada into the world economy. Industrial development strategy would help to ensure that the integration is on a basis which most benefits Canada.

Direct Government intervention with respect to foreign investmen can result in more exports, more domestic procurement, more R&D, and thus more employment. In itself, this is probably worth having, at least in the short-run.

But in the long-run, Canada will probably require more activity and employment in certain industries only — those in which Canada has some long-term capability and advantage It will not want it in all industries. It will also be essential for Canada to develop distinctiveness of its own. It is thus probably inevitable that the growing specialization of Canadian industry in the last 15 years or so will accelerate in the future. This process can be left largely to market forces (as influenced by general economic policies), or it can be shaped by an industrial development strategy. In this connection, of course, a screening process conscious of, and working within, the framework of an industrial development strategy is bound to be more effective than one which simply bargains for more of everything, whether or not Canada has a long-term future in the industry concerned.

Non-Economic Implications

Quite apart from such economic costs as are interwoven with the benefits of direct investment, there is a cultural and political impact of direct investment upon Canada. In some instances it may operate directly through, for example, foreign control of cultural activities, such as book publishing. This may be the kind of situation in which specific ownership rules for a particular sector are most appropriate.

More generally, the very large degree of direct investment does have an important bearing upon Canadian culture. The multinational enterprise is the purveyor of new technologies, which tend to have a levelling effect upon Canadian culture, and consequently to reduce the possibilities of creating a unique Canadian identity and culture. Direct investment also has an adverse impact upon entrepreneurial and innovative activity in Canada, with a resulting deleterious effect upon Canadian creativity.

With regard to the political impact, its main drawbacks are: it reduces Canadian options in industrial and related aspects of economic policy, pushing Canada towards continental integration; extraterritoriality; the drawing of foreign governments into Canadian affairs.

These all tend to constitute arguments in favour of diversifying Canada's external relationships and of building up Canada's relationship with other countries, whereas the current degree of U.S. investment probably has the opposite impact — hampering relationships with third countries.

7

ALTERNATIVE POLICY APPROACHES

THE SCREENING PROCESS

Introduction

The present part looks at three broad alternative approaches — all involving some degree of intervention and discrimination — to meet the problems and opportunities presented by foreign investment. While not mutually exclusive, these broad approaches are treated separately. The possibility of some combination of these three approaches is touched on in various points in this part. These three approaches are: the introduction of a screening process; the identification of further "key sectors" where Canadian ownership would be protected and foreign investment controlled; the introduction of compulsory Canadian shareholders (e.g. 51 per cent Canadian ownership) and fixed rules relating to the appointment of Canadian directors, Canadian managers, etc.

The pros and cons of each of these approaches is considered below. It is concluded that the introduction of a screening mechanism is potentially an approach that would involve no costs. Furthermore, it could make a positive contribution to the achievement of national economic objectives.

Nature and Objectives of the Screening Process

The analysis of foreign direct investment in this Memorandum suggests that the foreign investor's distinctiveness gives him an advantage in dealing with the Canadian economy and a "pool of benefits" which make investing in Canada attractive to him. This distinctiveness may be based on cheaper access to a factor of production such as capital or labour, technological superiority, or the achievement of significant economies of scale. Distinctiveness may also result from capacities unrelated to efficiency or superiority, such as possession of market power.

The screening authority would have the power to review foreign direct investment in Canada. Where such investment is based on the possession of some superiority or efficiency not available in Canada, the screening agency would bargain for better performance. It would seek to influence the quality and quantity of activities carried on in Canada, e.g. greater rationalization, research and development, exports, and procurement. Where foreign direct investment is adding nothing of significance to the Canadian economy, (e.g. where it is basically the extension of foreign market power into Canada), it would be blocked.

The screening authorities would also examine whether there are preferable alternative means of obtaining the distinctiveness, (e.g. licensing) or preferable alternative sources either in Canada or abroad.

In taking its decision, the screening authority would have to be guided by some criteria or guidelines. In general terms, its decisions would be guided by the Government's industrial strategy and considerations of industrial and economic efficiency. This could lead to some other potential investments being blocked. These criteria or guidelines are considered in greater detail later.

Basic Reasons for Screening Process

General environmental legislation such as tax, tariff and competition policy, even if significantly improved, is unlikely to maximize Canada's share of the investor's return on his distinctiveness.

An investor's distinctiveness is usually based on a capacity he developed in his home market. As pointed out, to a certain extent, it is beyond the reach of Canadian laws and policies. As long as international competitive structures are imperfect and as long as there is no international agency to regulate global markets, Canadian general economic policies can only go part of the way in capturing the benefits of direct investment in Canada. Direct intervention through the screening process is the only way of extracting further benefits which otherwise would be shared between the foreign investor and his home economy.

The screening process can focus attention on industries and cases which are important for Canadian economic development, and take into account Canada's bargaining position which will vary from industry to industry and case to case, i.e. its flexibility to adapt to different industries and different cases, and to changing conditions over time.

In the light of the Government's industrial strategy, the screening authorities would seek to secure the best possible deal from foreign investment, and to block its entry where it is not beneficial. It would be concerned with such factors as technology, the development of specialization, exports, imports, and research and product development. It would examine these factors in the light of their impact on such things as industrial efficiency and structure, the level of economic activity and employment, and the quality of goods and services in Canada. This requires a flexible instrument capable of examining particular cases. It is very difficult to carve out a particular sector or to formulate general rules which can be applied to all sectors and all firms covering such things as exports, imports, research and development, etc. This may be partly a reflection of limited knowledge of the industry, but is more likely the result of the fact that the critical variable in performance differs from industry to industry and case to case.

A screening mechanism would allow Canada to marshal and concentrate Canadian bargaining power to maximize benefits to Canada from foreign direct investment. It would allow Canada to collect its bargaining power in one agency established to deal with a potential foreign investor. It should be remembered that this investor has a distinctive strength based on technological superiority, on some other advantage, or on market power. The most effective way of moving more of the benefits from the investor's distinctive capacities to Canada is to concentrate Canadian bargaining power in one agency.

A screening process would also enable Canada to resist foreign direct investment which enjoys an arbitrary advantage, e.g. resulting from a foreign government incentive. Alternatively, it could bargain to obtain better performance in Canada and in effect move some of the benefits of the foreign government incentive to Canada. It could negotiate with the foreign investor to put pressure on his home government to reduce trade barriers on Canadian manufactures. At present, a foreign investor can play off one province against another and obtain grants from both the Federal and Provincial Governments. The screening process could not eliminate this type of "wheeling and dealing". It could, however, "neutralize" the effect of these grants in arriving at its final decision if it chose to do so.

A screening process would minimize "protectionism" which could prove costly to the Canadian economy. The delineation of key sectors to be protected from foreign investment or the introduction of precise formulae on such things as the extent of exports, the procurement of components, etc. would necessarily be arbitrary and consequently potentially economically costly. A screening process, if effectively administered, could avoid the economic costs potentially associated with blocking all direct investment, with blocking all direct investment in a particular industry regardless of its terms or accompanying benefits, (e.g. technology) or with establishing fixed percentages or standards for exports, procurement, etc. without regard for the economics of individual industries or cases.

The screening process would be able to take into account the existence of international investment, particularly the MNE, and use it to Canada's advantage.

The screening process would permit Canada to build into its industrial and general economic policies a recognition of the fact that a growing proportion of industry has a world-wide focus and multinational corporate links. The industrial policy of most governments has tended to lag behind this development. A screening process would enable Canada to accept the MNE as an efficient structure for some industries and seek to use its existence as a channel to bargain for more activity in Canada. In those industries or cases where foreign direct investment or the expansion of the MNE in Canada simply represents the extension of market power, the screening agency would be in a position to block it.

A screening process is a mechanism with which international business is familiar. Most countries have some power of control over direct investment. A number of governments have some type of screening process. The fact that businessmen are familiar with this type of mechanism makes it easier for Canada to use this approach.

The screening process would focus on business terms and conditions. In arriving at a decision, the screening authorities would focus on such things as the nature of the technology being introduced into Canada, the degree of specialization in the product line, exports, procurement, research and product development, etc. These are all factors with which businessmen are familiar and therefore would make the screening process an intelligible institution. The screening authorities would seek to make a good business deal on the basis of factors a businessman understands.

A screening process could take into account the surrounding environment of particular industries as positive policies develop indigenous capacities in these areas.

As positive policies in the areas of capital markets, technology, management, etc. take hold and effect changes in the environment for particular industries, the need for foreign direct investment in these industries will decline. The use of a screening mechanism, as opposed to the delimitation of key sectors or the introduction of across-the-board ownership rules, will be able to take this development into account.

The problems of a screening process include the uncertainty which the structure poses for the business community; the additional degree of intervention a screening process represents in the private sector; the power which it places in public hands; the political pressure which the capacity to make these decisions will invite; the regional and other particular interests which will feel thwarted by the screening authorities; and the difficulties in making the judgments involved.

Scope of Screening Authority

In considering the scope of the screening authority, the following questions are considered:

1. What specific corporate functions or activities will be screened, (exports, imports, research and development, etc.)?
2. What criteria or guidelines will be used by the screening authorities in arriving at their decisions?
3. What is the relationship of these guidelines to other Government programmes and priorities?
4. Does Canada have the bargaining power to use effectively a screening process?
5. What categories of activities will be considered, (e.g. takeovers, new investment, expansion of existing firms, etc.)?

This section deals with the first question only. Subsequent sections consider each of the other questions in turn.

In coming to a decision on a particular investment, the screening authorities will want to consider the following aspects of corporate structure and behaviour:

a. the nature of the product line and the extent of rationalization in the corporate organization;
b. the nature of the technology to be employed (in comparison with the technology available in Canada);
c. plans for research and development and product innovation in Canada;
d. export plans and market opportunities to be made available to the subsidiary including consideration of whether the subsidiary is to be excluded from certain export markets either because of the parent's global marketing strategy or because of the laws, policies or regulations of the parent's home government;
e. plans for sourcing materials, components, and services in Canada;
f. plans for expansion of the subsidiary;

    g. plans for the hiring of Canadian managers, and other employees, and the appointment of Canadian directors;

    h. capital structure and sources of financing (including the opportunity for equity participation by Canadians);

    i. the degree of processing of resources (if in the resource industries).

These factors are not all of equal importance. Their significance for Canadian economic development will vary from industry to industry and case to case. In weighing these factors, the screening agency has three possibilities: it can refuse the investment if nothing of significance is being added to the Canadian economy; it can permit the investment, subject to obtaining more benefits through bargaining; it can come to the decision that the investment is important for Canada but still bargain for greater benefits.

Bargaining could take place over some or all of the following factors:

    a. degree of rationalization including production for export markets, or the shifting to Canada of production of components for parents and affiliates abroad;

    b. the location of research and product development facilities in Canada;

    c. possible future expansion in Canada;

    d. degree of processing of raw materials in Canada.

To a lesser extent, bargaining could take place over the nature of the product line, or the nature of the technology to be used. An attempt could be made, for example, to obtain the use of more modern technology in Canada. Depending on the balance of payments situation or the domestic credit situation, bargaining may also take place over capital structure and sources of financing, e.g. the screening authorities may wish to urge the foreign investor to import all of his capital requirements. The use of Canadian managers and directors would normally not be a matter for bargaining but would be taken into account in the final cost/benefit judgment. The employment of Canadians in these positions is unlikely to have a significant impact on the behaviour of the foreign controlled firm but is of benefit because of the training it provides.

In arriving at its final cost/benefit judgment, the screening authorities will wish to consider whether equal benefits are available from a Canadian source. They would also consider the possibility of severing the foreign direct investment package and obtaining the distinctive capacity in a form other than through direct investment e.g. technology through licensing or in the form of a joint venture. The screening agency would also look at the possibility of obtaining the distinctive input from an alternative foreign source.

Each of the elements over which bargaining takes place represent an attempt by the screening agency to severe the direct investment package and obtain the distinctive capacity at a lower cost, e.g. by reducing or removing export restrictions, by requiring greater production or procurement in Canada where economic, etc. The most radical form of severance is the licensing of technology. A joint venture is a sort of half-way house between foreign direct investment and licensing. Whatever the particular method used to severe the package, it will normally give Canadian entrepreneurs and suppliers better opportunities to increase production and employment.

LICENSING AND JOINT VENTURES

The value of licensing and joint ventures lies in the fact that they may impose fewer restrictions on the activities within Canada and result in greater benefits to Canada from the activity in question. More generally, these techniques permit greater Canadian influence over the industrial activity involved while enjoying the advantages of the superior foreign inputs.

In the case of licensing, the general pattern is that the licensee is generally left some latitude in management, production, procurement, sale and pricing. The Canadian environment is left freer to "shop around" for various inputs including the pursuit of alternative sources of the technology if other sources exist or arise at a later date.

Licensing is in the Canadian interest where the purchaser can achieve superior terms for the transfer of the distinctiveness. To do this, the purchaser must have the capacity to select wisely and to operate and develop the "know-how" which is made available at arms length. The capacity of the transferee to develop a further unique distinctiveness is of importance since that would increase the benefits of arms length transfer.

Licensing does not normally lead to a continuous relationship between the seller and the Canadian transferee, whereas foreign direct investment ordinarily provides easy access to the latest developments. As a result, further development of the "know-how" which is transfered would have to be separately sought. The importance of this factor would influence the screening process in its preference for direct investment or licensing in different industries.

The foreign proprietor of the "know-how" will often favour direct investment as a technique of maximizing his benefits. If he lacks resources and can gain most of the benefits through licensing, he might favour this technique.

A joint venture is a half-way house between direct investment and arms length procurement of the distinctive input. The presence of a Canadian participant in the management of an enterprise can increase the benefits for Canada. The appropriateness of this technique and the extent to which it adds to the benefits for Canada will also vary from one setting to another.

Finding a Canadian partner with the requisite capacities to enter a joint venture may be difficult. The inputs which each partner has to make is particularly important if the joint venture is to survive, i.e. if they are very uneven, the prospects are less bright. Similarly, the more dynamic the setting, the more precarious is the joint venture as the distribution of responsibility and proceeds may become inappropriate over time. The likelihood of indigenous development by the joint venture and the degree of independence which it might achieve from the foreign participant will also affect the attitude of the screening process to the proposed joint venture.

The screening process should also remain alert to the possibilities of using contractual transfer techniques, e.g. the use of management contracts, assistance arrangements, temporary joint ventures, the participation of the CDC, etc., should all be kept in mind.

GUIDELINES OF SCREENING PROCESS

Making a cost/benefit judgement on a particular foreign direct investment involves the use of certain criteria or guidelines. Otherwise, the screening process could become an agent of incrementalism, i.e. bargaining for more exports, more procurement, more research and development, etc. regardless of its impact on industrial development. The screening authorities should work on the basis of an industrial strategy which would apply to both the screening authorities and other economic and industrial policies, e.g. trade policy. Until the Government has established which should be the basis for Canadian specialization, the screening process could aim at industrial efficiency, in order to maximize our international competitiveness and our domestic output for a given effort. The following framework could be used.

The guiding principle would be that Canada cannot do everything for itself, and must, therefore, specialize between industries and rationalize within those industries which are the bases of specialization. Such specialization and rationalization would assist the development of Canadian distinctiveness which would become sufficiently attractive internationally to generate high levels of employment. Implicit in this approach is the judgment that foreign investment would be welcome where it is compatible with Canadian objectives and where it constitutes a desirable and least costly technique of achieving certain results.

Increased economic activity and employment can be one of the major benefits of foreign direct investment. The screening agency should therefore also take into account the impact of a particular investment on these factors. It should also consider the actual and potential spill-over benefits such as the training of Canadian managers and labour. In weighing these factors, it is important that the agency not operate on the basis of incrementalism, but in accordance with the Government's industrial strategy and the other guidelines mentioned below.

A screening process could become a powerful additional instrument supporting the Government's determination to improve economic conditions in the slow growth regions of the country. The screening agency could be directed to award "plus" points for location in particular slow growth regions. This approach should allay the fears of some of the "have-not" provinces that believe that a foreign investment policy would protect the position of the "have" proinces, most of which benefitted greatly in the past from foreign direct investment. (The "have-not" provinces tend to believe that domestic capital markets and institutions do not serve their needs adequately.) On the other hand, an approach of this nature would likely cause a strong reaction in the "have" provinces. The fears of the "have" provinces could, to a certain extent, be alleviated if the screening agency takes into account as a negative factor, the amount of any grants given for regional location.

The aspects of corporate behaviour listed in the subsection on *Licensing and Joint Ventures* would thus be considered in terms of their impact on the following factors:

a. the Government's industrial strategy (to the extent articulated);
b. productivity and industrial efficiency, including technological development;
c. the level of economic activity and employment;
d. the geographic location within Canada and the potential contribution of the investment to reducing regional disparities;
e. other economic benefits, (e.g. training and other spill-over benefits);
f. the extent to which the foreign entrant will stimulate competitive market forces in Canada, including the impact on prices and the quality of goods and services available in Canada.

The use of these guidelines would lead to the treatment of foreign direct investment in four general ways.

In some industries, foreign direct investment would be dominant because it possesses some superior distinctiveness over Canadian firms which cannot be acquired via licence or through a joint venture. In these industries, the screening authorities would bargain with the investor over terms of entry. If more activity can be based in Canada economically, it would be sought. The screening authorities would seek a role for the Canadian subsidiary in the global corporate strategy if the industry were, in fact, international. Because the foreign investor's distinctive capacity is great in these cases, it must be recognized that bargaining may not result in substantial added benefits and that the investment will nonetheless be welcomed as a valuable one. In these circumstances, the screening agency may wish to recommend a tariff reduction as a means of keeping the foreign investor efficient.

In other industries, the distinctiveness may not be as great and Canadian controlled firms may exist that can develop it. In these cases, the screening authorities would seek to acquire the distinctive capacity through licence or promote the establishment of a joint venture with a Canadian firm. The foreign investment may be allowed in order to stimulate competition; alternatively, it may be blocked and tariffs lowered simultaneously.

In other industries, perhaps with both Canadian and foreign controlled firms, the screening authorities may determine that new foreign direct investment is not adding anything new, i.e. new technology, new markets or new competitive stimulus. The investment may even be detrimental, e.g. distort industrial priorities, have anti-competitive effects, etc. If nothing of value is being brought to Canada, the entry would be refused. This would not be motivated primarily by the desire to protect Canadian entrepreneurs but rather to maximze net benefits to Canada. This is least likely to occur in the case of new investment in manufacturing. It is most likely to occur in the case of takeovers or investment in the resource industries.

It follows that foreign investment would be resisted:
a. where the Canadian economy is strong so that foreign investment is not vital to economic development;
b. where foreign investment is based simply on the extension or entrenchment of market power in Canada;
c. where foreign investment distorts Canadian industrial priorities (perhaps because of foreign government incentives which cannot be effectively "neutralized" or captured);
d. where foreign investment has anti-competitive effects.

The ability to resist foreign direct investment depends to a large extent upon the existence of Canadian capacities. This serves to underline the importance of the positive aspects of the policy which is recommended in this Memorandum. The various positive measures should, over time, reduce the pressures of foreign investment. A foreign entrant who today possesses a superior distinctiveness may tomorrow be resisted or required to enter Canada via licence or joint venture. Improved Canadian capabilities should also increase the bargaining power of the screening agency and permit it to negotiate better arrangements. Similarly, policies designed to improve the general economic environment — making all industry more efficient regardless of ownership — would affect the extent to which the screening authorities have to bargain over certain elements. For example, the market itself might produce less fragmentation if more competitive conditions exist and lower production costs make it easier to attract foreign firms to undertake various activities in Canada.

There is a fourth category of industry which the Government may decide to reserve for Canadian controlled firms for non-economic reasons. Potential candidates are considered in the context of the discussion of key sectors in the section on *Foreign Exchange Controls*.

The guidelines suggested above envisage the screening process as a mechanism which would impose no costs on the Canadian economy and which would, potentially, increase economic efficiency. If the Government is prepared to countenance some economic cost (which could produce long-run benefits), it could graft a protectionist dimension on to the present policy proposals. For example, it could identify certain key sectors which would be protected for development by Canadian controlled firms or it could protect any industry where Canadian entrepreneurs are judged to be at the "take-off" point.

If more were known about the industries which the Government wishes to see develop in Canada, (i.e. if a detailed industrial strategy existed), it would be possible to add this protection of Canadian entrepreneurs without difficulty. In the absence of this knowledge, the screening process should probably be a non-protectionist mechanism. Protection of Canadian entrepreneurs can be built in at a later stage when the Government's industrial strategy is defined.

Relationship to Other Government Programmes and Priorities

There is a danger that pressures will develop to turn the screening process into a receptacle for the implementation of a wide variety of Government programmes and objectives. For example, particular interest groups might petition the screening agency not to permit a particular investment or takeover, unless the foreign investor undertakes to install certain anti-pollution devices; or to employ workers from a certain locale, or procure components from a certain plant to maintain employment; or to contribute to certain worthy community ventures, etc. Many of these pressures are already felt by the Government, but the existence of a screening agency would provide a new channel of access to the decision making process.

Pressures of this sort could destroy the effectiveness of the screening agency. They could lead to uneconomic decisions that would be very costly in both the short and the long-run. The screening agency should be protected from pressures of this sort. Its mandate should be to recommend to the Government acceptance or rejection of a particular foreign investment solely on the basis of the guidelines outlined in the previous subsection. If pressures develop, for example, to create or maintain jobs which are clearly uneconomic, the Government and the agency must have the determination to resist these pressures.

There is also the danger that the screening process will be required to reconcile a wide variety of political pressures unrelated to specific Government objectives. There are always pressures to protect certain interests, to favour specific groups, etc. Pressures will be brought to bear to support or reject particular entries or takeovers. Competitors will seek to keep a foreign investor out. The beneficiaries, (e.g. labour unions) will urge approval. Local M.P.'s, provincial governments and municipal authorities or community spokesmen will tend to support the particular foreign investment in their area. These pressures are likely to be less severe in the case of takeovers since there is an existing Canadian operation in place. A strict mandate to make recommendations on the basis of the guidelines suggested above should help the screening authorities to resist these sorts of pressures.

The latter problem might be alleviated by making the screening authorities independent of the Government, but this possibility raises a number of serious problems of its own. This Memorandum does not support such an approach. It is discussed more fully below in the subsection: *Summary and Conclusions.*

Bargaining Power

If the screening process is to be able to secure greater benefits from foreign direct investment, it must have real bargaining power. The law must give it the authority to refuse a potential entry or takeover without either finding a comparable Canadian operation to fill the void or imposing on some public body the obligation of making the investment. In the manufacturing industries, Canada's main bargaining lever will be the size and affluence of the Canadian market. While not enormous, it provides an attractive investment for a foreign manufacturer, especially if the costs of developing his product for his home market have been "sunk". His desire to enter and exploit the Canadian market is our main bargaining strength. The screening agency's hand will be reinforced by the fear that failure to come to terms may allow a competitor to gain an advantage. While Canada's bargaining strength in the manufacturing field is not overwhelming, there is some scope which has not been utilized in the past.

The Canadian authorities could probably hold out for most in the resource based industries. Unlike manufacturing, where the investor possesses the distinctive capacity, in resources the advantage is in Canadian hands. Access to a stable long-term supply of raw materials is often an important consideration for a processor who has tied up large amounts of capital in his processing and fabricating facilities, and has developed his global market position over a long period of time. It is unlikely that the screening authorities will be able to change the location of processing and fabricating facilities in the short run in many instances. But it is in a position to bargain for the location of the next expansion in Canada. While foreign markets have barriers to imports of fabricated goods, Canadian insistence on such manufacturing would lead to pressures on those markets to lower the barriers.

Canada's bargaining power will vary from mineral to mineral depending on the world supply and demand situation. The Government's review of mineral policy should identify those areas where Canada's bargaining position is strongest as a guide to the screening authorities.

What Will Be Screened?

The screening authorities could be required to examine one more of the following:

a. takeovers;
b. new investment;
c. licences and franchises;
d. expansions of existing foreign controlled firms in Canada;
e. foreign controlled firms in Canada that are not expanding;
f. Canadian multinational companies.

These possibilities are considered in turn.

FOREIGN TAKEOVERS

The screening authority would look at foreign takeovers of Canadian controlled firms (subject perhaps to a threshold size) according to the general guidelines relating to all foreign investment set out above. The screening agency would also review the acquisition of a foreign controlled firm operating in Canada by another foreign controlled firm. Briefly, an assessment would be made of the advantages of the proposed takeover; e.g. new technology, market access, competitive thrust, export and import plans, proposed location of R & D and other activities, methods of financing, management plans, etc. If little or no contribution is made to the industry by the foreign participation, it would be blocked. If superior terms were possible, the agency would negotiate for superior terms.

The approach suggested in this Memorandum has two basic underlying propositions:

a. the government ought not to adopt the posture of being a buyer of last resort in cases of foreign takeovers. It should simply prohibit undesirable acquisitions as it does unacceptable mergers generally;
b. the foreign takeover policy cannot hinge on a requirement of finding an alternative Canadian buyer on comparable terms, since to do so would seriously undermine any takeover policy.

It must be acknowledged that this approach will, occasionally, place the individual Canadian seller in a less favourable position as the group of potential purchasers would be somewhat narrowed. This of course also happens under competition policy, the Bank Act, the Broadcasting Act, etc. Furthermore, this limitation will affect individual proprietors in very few cases because of the size criterion and because acquisitions of smaller firms are more likely to be allowed. The rules would be declared clearly in advance and the business community would be given time to adapt to the new situation.

A proposed takeover also offers the opportunity of intervening to find a Canadian buyer either in the case of a proposed foreign takeover of a Canadian owned firm, or of a foreign owned firm which is changing hands. The screening authority would be encouraged to make such efforts even in cases where it would not ultimately block a foreign purchase. In fact, consideration might be given to an appropriate prescribed delay between a proposed foreign takeover and its completion during which public notice of the intended purchase would be given to permit a Canadian buyer to come forward.

A time period could be provided for the screening agency to declare its position — e.g., 60 days from the date on which all required information had been submitted. Once the agency declared its intention to oppose the takeover or to bargain over its terms, negotiations would begin. These could not be subject to any defined statutory time period without undermining the bargaining position of the agency.

Under the revisions to the Combines Investigation Act, an acquisition of a Canadian firm by a foreign interest will have to meet certain conditions.

Firstly, the general merger provisions empower the Tribunal to examine mergers which "significantly lessen competition". Such a merger would be prohibited unless it resulted in efficiencies, a substantial part of which were likely to be transmitted to the market place. A foreign takeover would be subject to these general rules.

Secondly, since a foreign takeover might not *lessen* competition from a previous level but still be detrimental to competition, a further set of rules would be applied by the Tribunal. The grounds for having these additional rules are basically that a foreign takeover can create or entrench market dominance of the acquired firm in Canada; that the influence of a foreign cartel or oligopoly may be introduced into Canada by the takeover reducing the competitive independence of the acquired firm; or that the takeover could lead to a restriction of production or exports by the Canadian firm. In each case, the defence applicable to Canadian mergers would be possible, namely, that the acquisition would lead to a significant improvement in efficiency with a substantial part of the benefits being transmitted to the market place.

These criteria will remove some takeovers from the screening process by virtue of the fact that they are harmful to domestic competition and have no redeeming virtue in creating new efficiencies. A foreign takeover, especially of a large Canadian firm, is a foreign investment which is least likely to introduce benefits into the economy. It frequently involves a simply change of owners with little or no improvement through economies of scale, new capacity, new technology, new employment or increased competition.

Nevertheless, the rules of competition policy would only block those takeovers which had an adverse impact on competition. They do not consider the further question whether the proposed takeover is *adding* positive economic benefits.

Competition policy would direct the thrust of foreign investment toward those firms which would be more likely to stimulate competition and efficiency, i.e. small or weaker firms. However, takeovers which were not blocked might still be of no benefit to Canada. New investment which might be undertaken as an alternative to a takeover might similarly be of no benefit to Canada. These latter two forms of investment would be considered by the screening process.

This procedure of applying a competitive rationale to foreign takeovers, prior to subjecting them to the screening process, will increase the number of foreign acquisitions which are dealt with by predetermined criteria enforced through an independent adjudicative agency. Fewer takeovers will be left for the more discretionary role of the screening process. The screening process, in blocking takeovers which add nothing of value to Canada or in bargaining for greater benefits, will undoubtedly examine more closely the takeover of large Canadian firms.

While this procedure involves two public bodies, this cannot be avoided without removing all consideration of foreign takeovers from competition policy, or all takeovers from the jurisdiction of the screening process. Neither of these alternatives is desirable. Foreign takeovers should not be treated more favourably than Canadian acquisitions under competition policy. They must, therefore, be subject to some competitive policy scrutiny. On the other hand, it would be potentially confusing to have the screening authorities administer the competition policy for foreign takeovers since conflicting interpretations of competition policy could arise. Furthermore, the screening process envisaged in this Memorandum is not an independent adjudicative agency which is the model applied to competition policy. The alternative of not reviewing takeovers through a screening process would frustrate the objective of blocking those foreign takeovers which add nothing of benefit to Canada and of bargaining with the would-be investor to achieve improved performance.

The solution would seem to lie in having the foreign purchaser apply to the screening authorities for approval and having those authorities notify the Competition Tribunal. The screening process would conduct its preliminary investigations while the Tribunal deliberated over the takeover. If the Tribunal did not oppose the takeover, the screening process would be able to enter into discussions with the foreign investor immediately, thus reducing any delays. The foreign investor would make only the only application to the screening process thus providing him with one point of contact with the Canadian Government.

It should be stressed that, as is the case with mergers generally, not every foreign takeover would raise doubts with the Tribunal. It would be the acquisition of large Canadian firms which would come under question. These acquisitions are the ones to be discouraged. Foreign investors will know these rules and set their acquisition or entry policies accordingly. Consequently, only a few foreign takeovers can be expected to involve two full steps of examination. They would usually be the ones which are particularly suspect from the perspective of Canadian interests.

NEW FOREIGN INVESTMENT

The approach to new foreign investment would be basically the same as that set out above for foreign takeovers. All new foreign direct investments would have to be notified to the screening agency, but many would be likely to proceed without further action by the agency. The focus of concern would be that of direct controlling foreign investment over a certain size.

The guidelines for screening processes set out above would apply to new direct investment. In addition, the screening agency could give consideration to the alternatives of a joint venture with a Canadian partner. the licensing of an independent Canadian entrepreneur, or the acquisition of the distinctive input from another foreign source. This means that the screening agency must have some technological know-how and the cooperation of industry in reaching its conclusions. The agreement to a joint venture or a licensing agreement would not obviate the need for screening and bargaining, but would be viewed positively by the agency in its analysis.

The agency would have a negotiating mandate to get the best terms possible for Canada from a proposed investment where that investment is potentially advantageous for Canada. Similarly, it would be open to the agency to block the entry if its evaluation or bargaining led to the conclusion that the net benefits to Canada were not significant or were negative.

LICENSING, FRANCHISING, AND LONG-TERM SUPPLY CONTRACTS

The kinds of restraints to which the screening guidelines are directed can be imposed on Canadian business through techniques other than direct investment. Licensing agreements in which the proprietor has an advantage can lead to similar constraints on Canadian activity as noted earlier in the section on *Technology*. Franchising of distributors or manufacturers can embody limitations on managerial discretion and the potential for various activities. Similarly, long-term supply contracts, particularly in resources, can tie the hands of Canadian producers and preclude their developing new activities in Canada, e.g. further processing. To preclude or screen direct investment without examining these contractual control control techniques leaves some scope for circumvention of government objectives in those cases where this form of business relationship is viable and in the interests of the immediate parties.

Even where this form of contractual relationship is not an attempt to circumvent the screening process, there is merit in attempting to enhance the bargaining position of the Canadian "buyer" or in otherwise improving the terms of operation in Canada. In many circumstances the agency might want to encourage this "arms length" method of securing foreign inputs and assistance, but the agency would not want to ignore the nature of the terms struck. The foreign licensor is in the position of a single seller facing a number of fragmented buyers. The intervention of the screening agency would help reduce the ability of the licensor to play off one potential licensee against another. It would not seem sufficient to depend on the private bargaining strength and objectives of the Canadian businessman to serve the public interest on the issues of concern to the screening agency.

Within these alternative forms of new foreign control (takeovers, new investment, and licensing and franchising), there is a greater likelihood that takeovers will be blocked than will new investment or licensing. While takeovers can add new inputs of considerable benefit to Canada and release resources for other uses in Canada, it is expected that under these guidelines fewer takeovers will appear attractive to the screening authorities than will new investments. New investments tend to face a stiffer test in the market place than takeovers. Similarly, fewer takeovers of large and established Canadian firms would appear attractive than would acquisitions of smaller or clearly inefficient firms.

EXPANSION OF FOREIGN CONTROLLED FIRMS

Since the foreign controlled sector of Canadian industry is very large and growing from internal sources, the issue of the expansion of such firms must be considered. In principle, a new investment by a firm in Canada is fundamentally no different from one made by a new entrant to Canada.

It is possible to provide for screening of:

a. expansions in new sectors or industries;
b. "major" new expansions in existing activities;
c. "new issues" which draw on domestic or foreign capital markets to fund expanded activity.

To curtail ordinary growth would disadvantage foreign controlled firms since an inability to grow would reduce their competitiveness. The focus of concern should be to secure terms from existing foreign controlled firms which are comparable to those bargained with new entrants by takeover and new investment.

There are at least three reasons for screening the expansion of existing foreign controlled firms. Firstly, they constitute a large and growing segment of the Canadian manufacturing and resource industries. A foreign ownership policy that ignored this fact could be ineffective as a means of increasing domestic control of the natural economic environment. Secondly, existing foreign controlled corporations could be used to circumvent the screening agency. If a would-be foreign entrant wants to avoid screening, he might be able to make an arrangement with a foreign firm at present in Canada (either one that it owns or one belonging to another foreigner) to undertake the new project, perhaps in an entirely unrelated industry. Lastly, the bargaining strength of the agency might be reduced if applicants can point to existing competitors who are not subject to the various constraints on behaviour by virtue of having entered prior to the policy coming into force.

The expansion into new industries by an existing foreign controlled firm in Canada is closest to a new entry. If the expansion were to occur via merger, the transaction would qualify as a foreign takeover and be subject to screening. If it were to occur through new investment, it would seem that screening ought to be possible. Furthermore, as noted above, this technique could be a means of frustrating the screening of new foreign investment in Canada if a foreign interest makes a deal with a foreign interest having a Canadian subsidiary.

Screening major new expansions impinges considerably more severely on the operations of existing foreign controlled firms in Canada. In substance, it raises the broader question of controlling the activities of existing foreign controlled firms in accordance with the guidelines of the screening authority. The use of the concept of "major expansions" is, in fact, simply a trigger for a review of existing foreign controlled firms. However, from the Government's point of view, it is a convenient trigger since the screening agency would have some bargaining power — i.e. the capacity to refuse permission for the expansion.

The logic of the screening process and the objectives it seeks to realize are as relevant to existing foreign controlled firms as they are to new entrants. Failure to screen such expansions would give a preference to existing foreign controlled firms over potential new entrants, a fact which may be undesirable for industrial development and competitive reasons. At the same time, if foreign controlled firms were not subject to review at the time of a major expansion the screening authority might find it more difficult to bargain with potential new entrants, who could claim that they will be disadvantaged compared to existing firms with which they will have to compete.

The concept of "new issues" is basically an alternative triggering device for screening the expansion of existing firms. Its advantage lies in providing a point of intervention that is likely to be easier to explain politically, viz., an issue in Canadian capital markets may be displacing a potential Canadian user of those funds. An issue floated on foreign capital markets can, in certain circumstances, also displace potential Canadian users of Canadian financial (and other) resources. Thus, it would be necessary to screen both Canadian and foreign issues by foreign controlled firms if this approach were taken.

This technique is likely to give a preference to a firm having internal resources within Canada or from its parent. It would also lead to attempts to transfer funds to the subsidiary from affiliates abroad, perhaps in non-equity forms (e.g. through transfer pricing) in order to avoid the screening mechanism. In view of these complications, if expansion is to be screened, it would seem preferable to do so directly.

EXISTING FOREIGN CONTROLLED FIRMS NOT EXPANDING

The broader question of screening existing foreign controlled firms, regardless of planned expansion in order to secure closer compliance with the guidelines of the screening authority, raises difficult questions. Once again, the logic of the screening process applies. This is particularly true in sectors where new foreign investment or takeovers are not too likely to occur, i.e. where the sector currently has most of the potential foreign investors already located in Canada. To avoid screening these firms does, as noted above, favour the existing firms over new entrants — a phenomenon which has potentially adverse "protectionist" implications.

It should be recognized that a policy which seeks to screen the existing foreign controlled firms (whether or not they are expanding) is likely to meet strong opposition from these firms. They will argue that the screening mechanism has retroactive impact, that it discriminates against foreign controlled firms, and that the Government is changing the rules of the game in a substantial way. It is to be expected that they will enlist the support of their home government for their claims.

In summary, the economic arguments for screening existing foreign controlled firms are strong whether they are expanding into new industries, expanding in their own industry, or merely subsisting in their own industry. The arguments are particularly forceful in the case of firms expanding into new industries since such expansions closely parallel new entry either in the form of new direct investment or takeover. Furthermore. the failure to screen expansion into new industries could lead to easy circumvention of the screening process.

The economic arguments for screening expansion in the same industry and for examining the performance of non-expanding firms are as persuasive as the arguments for screening new investment. But the political arguments against screening non-expanding firms and firms expanding in the same industry are also strong. Screening expansion in the same industry or in firms that are not expanding has considerable overtones of retroactivity and discrimination. While tax and tariff charges might be regarded as retroactive, they rarely discriminate in favour of Canadian controlled firms.

If the Government decides not to screen existing foreign controlled firms, it may wish to consider announcing that foreign controlled firms in an industry will be expected to perform over time to the performance guidelines negotiated with the new entrants. Otherwise they would be brought formally under the screening authority.

Thus, in dealing with existing foreign controlled firms the Government seems to face the following alternatives in descending order of economic effectiveness and ascending order of political acceptability:

    a. screen all existing foreign controlled firms whether they are expanding or not;

b. screen only foreign controlled firms that are expanding either in their own industry or into a new industry;

c. screen only foreign controlled firms expanding into a new industry;

d. screen foreign controlled firms at points where the Government is being asked for some kind of assistance;

e. publicize the types of decisions reached by the screening authorities in the case of takeovers, new investment from abroad, or in licensing and franchising agreements and use moral suasion to try to obtain equivalent beháviour from other firms in the industry.

CANADIAN CONTROLLED MULTINATIONAL FIRMS

While the analysis of this Memorandum has focused on foreign controlled firms, it was noted that Canadian firms can, by exporting capital, truncate their Canadian operations in much the same way as foreign controlled corporations. Canadian firms which mature to a multinational structure begin to reveal the symptoms of being influenced by their larger markets abroad, e.g. Canadian multinational enterprises such as Massey-Ferguson, frequently appear to be little different from their foreign controlled counterparts operating in Canada. This suggests that the Government should be cautious in pursuing a policy of developing Canadian multinationals even in industries where the MNE is the most efficient form of operation. It also suggests that many of the guidelines applying to foreign controlled firms should be extended to such firms despite their Canadian ownership.

Periodic Review

Consideration should be given to the possibility of periodically re-examining the terms of entry into Canada. Conditions change and the terms set might no longer be compatible with Canadian interests. This is distinct from surveillance and enforcement of compliance with the terms set in agreement with the screening agency which is discussed in the following section.

The screening agency should have the power to vary the terms of entry and to include a provision that the terms set would be subject to re-examination at some specified date. Direct investments in natural resources might be prime candidates for this sort of periodic reassessment. This type of provision is not unusual in business relationships. It is consistent with what the screening agency is to attempt to do, i.e. to strike a good business deal from the Canadian public perspective Care would have to be taken to avoid having the foreign entrant extract more onerous benefits from his Canadian operations more rapidly, due to the uncertainties as to the terms which might emerge from renegotiations.

It is conceivable, of course, that conditions might change so as to reduce the bargaining position of the Canadian authorities, but a business judgment must be made on this point at the time of entry. Fixed terms of entry in perpetuity is neither necessary as a business proposition, nor likely to be in Canada's long-run interests.

A decision by the Government to screen expansion of existing firms would obviate the need for this type of periodic review in some cases. It would not pick up existing foreign controlled firms that are not expanding.

Establishment of the Screening Agency

A screening agency could be established as either an independent adjudicative tribunal or an administrative agency responsible to a Minister.

An independent tribunal could be required to apply statutory criteria in specific cases subject perhaps to the possibility of Cabinet direction through Order-in-Council. Appeals might be authorized to Cabinet on matters of general principle or broad policy but not on the findings in specific cases. This would involve placing enormous power over the future direction of the Canadian nation in the hands of an independent body. On the other hand, it would remove Ministers from responsibility and involvement. Furthermore, it would permit the Federal Government to point out to the provinces that their standing before the agency would be no different than that of the Federal Government.

An alternative form of independent tribunal would be the establishment of a Federal-Provincial agency which would give the particular province affected a role in the decision making process. The advantage of this approach is obvious — the provinces would be more likely to accept a foreign ownership policy in whose implementation they have an important voice.

Against the advantages of an independent tribunal, whether or not it is constituted on a Federal-Provincial basis, must be weighed the disadvantages. The negotiating responsibilities and the breadth of the issues which must be taken into account suggest that an independent tribunal would be inappropriate. It would be extremely difficult for the Government to delegate responsibility over the future direction of the economy to a body not directly responsible to Parliament and the people.

If it is decided to opt for an agency responsible to Cabinet, the question arises whether it should report to a single Minister or to a statutory committee of Cabinet. The designation of a single Minister might reduce the political pressures on the agency and increase the likelihood that its decisions would be made solely on the basis of the operative guidelines. The Minister would, of course, consult his colleagues in the case of important decisions. If it is thought that the decisions involved are too broad, and that they raise too many inter-departmental and regional considerations to be left to a single Minister, it could be required that he be supported by a statutory committee of Cabinet. This latter alternative is probably the preferable one.

Short of involving the provinces formally in the actual decision of the agency (a procedure which would put a provincial representative in the impossible position of trying to serve both his government and a federal Minister), it would be possible to send a copy of the foreign investor's application to the relevant province for comments. There would, in any event, have to be close liaison between the Federal and Provincial Governments at both Ministerial and official levels if the agency is to work.

If Ministers decide to have a Ministerial agency, the question arises whether it should be assigned to a Minister with departmental resonsibilities or a Minister without Portfolio, e.g. a Minister of State. In either case, if it is decided to have a statutory committee of Cabinet, the Minister would be chairman of this committee.

There seem to be a number of reasons for prefering a Minister without departmental responsibilities. Firstly, such a Minister would not have any particular axe to grind. He could be expected to apply the guidelines more impartially than a Minister who must combine his foreign investment responsibilities with other duties. Secondly, during the early stages, until the statutory committee and the agency have dealt with a number of cases which will allow more decisions to be taken in the agency, the Minister can expect to have a heavy workload. Lastly, it is likely that the Minister will have to spend a considerable amount of his time receiving representations and discussing particular applications, especially in the early life of the agency.

Summary and Conclusions

On the basis of the evidence on the relative performance of Canadian and foreign controlled firms, this Memorandum does not recommend that the Government use Canadian ownership as a viable proxy for better performance. It recommends a more cautious approach, viz., looking directly at the performance of foreign controlled firms through a screening mechanism.

A screening process would give the Government a flexible institutional technique for dealing with the major problems of foreign direct investment and the growing importance of the MNE: truncation, the distortion of industrial priorities, export restrictions, import propensities, the location of research and product development, etc. It would allow the Government to marshal and concentrate Canadian bargaining power in dealing with foreign investors. It could pursue greater Canadian participation through licensing or joint ventures. It could also promote a policy of geographic diversification through the search for alternative sources of the distinctive input.

The screening process must be regarded as part of industrial policy. In making decisions, it would use guidelines based on the Government's industrial strategy, considerations of industrial efficiency, industrial activity and employment, regional location, and competition. It would have to work along with other policies and programmes aimed at these objectives. It would have to avoid becoming a receptacle for Government objectives which should be met by other policies.

In addition to bargaining for better performance, the agency would block foreign direct investment in certain cases. But the agency envisaged would not be a protectionist mechanism. It would only block direct investment when it did not accord with the Government's industrial priorities, when it was based solely on market power and thus brought no net benefits, or when Canadian entrepreneurs could do the job. It allows a check against errors in judgment about the ability of the Canadian economy to perform because the possibility of foreign entry to take advantage of any gaps is always present. Thus, the screening process would "protect" areas of basic Canadian strength from arbitrary displacement. It would rely on the Government's positive policies to develop additional areas of strength through improvements in capital markets, technology policy, competition policy, etc. Over time, as Canadian strengths developed, more foreign direct investment would probably be blocked or displaced in the ordinary working of the market place. The screening process as envisaged thus presents a challenge to the business community and to Canadian Governments to secure better performance from the economy.

A screening process which blocks direct investment only where it does not accord with industrial priorities or where Canada has its own capacities will not significantly increase Canadian ownership. It will maintain existing Canadian ownership where this is efficient. It will also increase the benefits of foreign direct investment. By sifting out anti-competitive direct investment and takeovers, it should reduce the proportion of foreign ownership in the economy in the long-run. The burden for increasing the proportion of Canadian ownership falls mainly on positive policies related to strengthening Canadian entrepreneurship, capital markets, technology and other supporting policies.

This analysis is not meant to imply that ownership is unimportant. Ownership can be important in avoiding truncation. Avoiding truncation is important in those industries fundamental to the realization of the Government's objectives. Furthermore, the location of the decision making function in Canada may be important if the Government is to avoid the type of problem it had with RCA over Telesat. However, the industries where Canada should avoid truncation or ensure that decision making is located here can only be suggested by a general industrial strategy.

The screening process recommended is basically a "cost-free" approach. There may be some degree of residual protection in the period of delay before Canadian entrepeneurs fill a gap where a foreign investment has been blocked. But this is likely to be minimal if the Government is prepared to countenance some cost (which should in the long run produce benefits), a protectionist role could be assigned to the screening agency, i.e. the protection of Canadian entrepreneurship by blocking direct investment in certain industries. Such a decision should only be taken on the basis of an overall industrial strategy which identifies industries where the short run costs of protection will probably be more than compensated by the long run benefits. This, however, is not the policy that is being recommended here. The possibility of adding a protectionist dimension to the screening process is considered more fully in the section on *Key Sectors*.

The screening agency could examine takeovers, new investment, licensing and franchising, expansion of existing foreign controlled firms, existing foreign controlled firms even if they are not expanding, and Canadian MNEs. The minimum coverage for a meaningful policy is probably takeovers, new investment and licensing and franchising. The screening of expansion of existing foreign controlled firms into new industries is probably also desirable. The screening authorities would not look at all cases. They would focus only on those of economic significance.

In addition to its bargaining function, the screening mechanism would also:

a. have the power to conduct investigation of particular industries or practices at the request of the Minister;
b. advise the Government on foreign ownership policy;
c. gather information necessary for purposes of identifying foreign control; and
d. perform an advisory consultative function in relation to Government policies and programmes affecting the foreign controlled sector.

Of the alternative administrative structures, the establishment of an agency responsible to the Minister and a statutory committee of Cabinet is probably the most practical.

FOREIGN EXCHANGE CONTROLS

A possible alternative approach to a screening process would be the implementation of full-blown foreign exchange controls. Such controls exist on the statute books of almost all western countries except Canada, the U.S., Germany, and Switzerland, but they are not in active use in many cases. Some countries that do not have foreign exchange control legislation have in fact used the technique of influencing international capital flows quite extensively, e.g., the U.S.

Mechanics

A foreign exchange control is normally used to control payments to foreigners for balance of payments reasons. It can be used to control capital flows, invisible payments, merchandise trade, or some combination of these three. Normally, all receipts from exports and other sources must be surrendered to the control authorities. The available supply of foreign exchange is then allocated to various buyers according to certain criteria related to national needs.

The foreign control agency usually authorizes certain private financial institutions to engage in foreign exchange transactions subject to the rules which it sets down. In the case of Canada, the banks would probably be the sole authorized institution. It is the banks that now run the foreign exchange market. The banks would be legally required to implement exchange control regulations and to compile statistical data as needed by the agency.

Measures Which Could be Implemented Through a Foreign Exchange Control Apparatus

The principal value of a foreign exchange control system is that i puts the Government in a position to have a more independent balance of payments and monetary policy. Less account need be taken of the international environment and more emphasis can be given to tailoring monetary policy to domestic economic needs. For example, a foreign exchange control would permit scrutiny of portfolio investment in Canada. Thus, it would give the Federal Government the power to regulate the foreign borrowings of provinces, municipalities and corporations. This latter power would, of course, facilitate implementation of balance of payments policy by enabling the Government to fight upward pressure on the exchange rate at times when the rate was considered to be undesirably high. Similarly, the power to restrict exports of portfolio capital at a time of undesirable downward pressure on the exchange rate would be possible.

Too much emphasis must not be put on the potential for increase economic independence resulting from exchange controls, particular for an internationally oriented economy such as Canada's. Trade flows, including those arising from foreign direct investment which passed the screening process, would have to be serviced or underlying economic activity would be affected. Speculative flows and more discretionary expenditures could be controlled to the extent that they are distinguishable from basic trade flows. The ability to control the movement of large amounts of speculative money would be a particularly valuable tool for the Government. However, it must be realized that it is difficult to distinguish speculative from non-speculative flows.

Regulating foreign borrowings by the provinces would be a major political decision. This Memorandum does not deal with the pros and cons of such a measure. However, it should be noted that exchange controls would provide an additional instrument for effective economic management.

Foreign exchange control would also permit the Government to scrutinize and to approve all payments between affiliated firms. Thus, authority would be available for verifying the transfer of prices for goods and services, the level of dividend payments, and so on. This could help to ensure that there is no circumvention of the Income Tax Act and other federal statutes which provide authority for the collection of revenues. Exchange controls could also be used to help achieve other Government objectives, e.g., a higher rate of employment by forcing procurement in Canada.

However, it is questionable that this indirect method of enforcing other statutes or of achieving Government objectives is desirable. It would seem that transfer pricing and other problems should be dealt with in a direct fashion under the relevant statute or Government programme.

Foreign Exchange Controls as an Alternative to a Screening Process

A foreign exchange control system, in its conventional sense, is not a viable alternative to a screening process. It could not perform many of its functions. A screening process, as envisaged in this Memorandum, would examine takeovers new investment and licensing and other contractual arrangements. It might perhaps also screen the expansion of existing foreign controlled firms into new industries and provide advice to Government agencies giving loans or grants to foreign controlled firms. It would search for alternatives to direct investment such as licensing arrangements. The screening process would bargain for better performance or block foreign direct investment in cases where there were no significant economic benefits for Canada. A traditional foreign exchange control system would not have all of these capacities. For example, it could not screen a foreign direct investor who raised funds in Canada; it could not screen licensing and other forms of contractual arrangements. It could only get at foreign direct investment using Canadian funds or licensing arrangements when and if payments were made abroad. Attempts to influence the terms and conditions of the arrangements at this point would create difficult problems of retroactivity.

This does not mean that a screening process could not be built onto a foreign exchange control system. This in fact is what has happened in many countries. Since almost all foreign direct investment involves some international transactions at some point in time, the foreign investor normally seeks prior approval of the foreign exchange control agency. The existence of foreign exchange controls then becomes a trigger mechanism to introduce the bargaining process with the foreign investor. This bargaining could be done either by the agency or by other arms of the Government. To the extent that prior approval is sought, the foreign exchange control agency in fact becomes a screening process with the threat of denial of foreign exchange as a sanction in the bargaining process.

Most of the problems associated with using foreign exchange controls as a method of controlling direct investment arise from the fact that exchange controls are basically designed to regulate the volume of payments to non-residents. Exchange controls are not concerned with factors such as the level of activity in Canada, the level and quality of research and product development, the degree of processing, export and procurement plans, etc. which are of vital concern to a screening agency.

Conclusions

A traditional foreign exchange control is not a viable alternative to a screening process because it is basically a balance of payments mechanism designed to control payments to non-residents. It could not perform many of the functions required of a screening agency. A screening function could be superimposed on a foreign exchange control mechanism but this would be a cumbersome and indirect way of implementing the Government's objectives in the field of foreign direct investment.

KEY SECTORS: AN ALTERNATIVE POLICY APPROACH

Approach to Key Sectors

In its decision in March 1970, Cabinet directed that further consideration be given to establishing a "check list of criteria identifying essential national interests, in the light of which decision regarding the importance of Canadian control in sectors of the economy could be judged." Cabinet also requested "proposals for key sectors in the economy in which Canadian control might be maintained."

There are two alternative viewpoints which can be taken in respect of the "key sector" concept. The first is that this concept, rather than the screening process, should become the fundamental cornerstone for future Canadian policy on the foreign ownership issue; i.e., the screening process should be dropped. Policy would then be based exclusively upon the criteria which would be decided upon by the Government, and sectors would be reserved for Canadian control pursuant to those agreed criteria. The second viewpoint is that the key sector concept should be a supplement to a general policy based upon a screening process, but should not itself be the main element in the policy.

It is concluded here that the former approach is a less desirable alternative than a screening process — because it is potentially much more costly in economic terms. This is for several reasons. To begin with, a key sector approach would be less effective than a screening process in providing the Government with a tool for influencing the economic environment, since ownership is not a sufficient proxy and would not secure valuable foreign inputs. Secondly, it would also be less effective in protecting the Government's industrial priorities. Thirdly, it could prove unduly protectionist of Canadian business management and entrepreneurship, leading to inefficiencies which might in turn require additional tariff protection against imports. Fourthly, a key sector approach is a less satisfactory response than a screening process to the emergence on the world scene of the multinational enterprise, with its strong bargaining power vis-a-vis national governments. Finally, some of the sectors which might prove eventually to be "key sectors" cannot be readily identified on the basis of the economic criteria discussed below, except by case-by-case study over a period of time. They would, however, remain subject to the possibility of change over time as the circumstances dictate. This kind of case-by-case analysis would need to be done by some sort of agency not unlike the screening agency described previously. In effect, screening is a process for evolving key sectors on a flexible basis over time. The sectors for Canadian ownership and control would flow out of the screening process.

On the other hand, the "key sector" approach could prove to be a useful supplement to the overall screening process approach. Within the framework of a general policy based on a screening process, and guided by the economic guidelines proposed in the section on the screening process, the Government could decide that rules should be made to guide the screening agency to support or to have a bias for Canadian control in certain sectors; and in other sectors of the economy, the Government could remove all discretion from the agency and legislate Canadian control where this was felt to be essential. These ideas will be elaborated below.

Definition

In essence, a key sector policy is a policy which emphasizes "Canadian control" of Canadian firms. In contrast, the screening process discussed above focused more upon the performance of firms. In this context, "Canadian control" implies sufficient Canadian ownership of the shares of a company that the management effectively rests in Canadian hands (whether equity ownership in Canada is 100 per cent or 40 per cent).

On the other hand, unlike the alternatives discussed in the next section, which deals with the desirability of a 50 or 51 per cent ownership for *all* Canadian firms of significant size, the key sector approach focuses upon Canadian control only in respect of certain designated sectors, not across the entire economy.

Over the past 15 years, the Federal Government has from time to time identified particular sectors of the economy which it wished to reserve wholly or partly for Canadian control. In the past, the essence of the concept of a key sector has been that there is something intrinsically special about a portion of the economy which makes it either essential or desirable that the firms in it be wholly or largely subject to Canadian conrol; that certain objectives of the Canadian Government and people cannot be fulfilled satisfactorily without the presence of Canadian controlled firms in the sector.

To a substantial degree, these objectives have in the past been largely non-economic. Thus, broadcasting, magazines, periodicals and newspapers have been designated to one degree or another as key sectors.

Even the decisions to make the banks and other federally-incorporated institutions key sectors seem not to have been based entirely on strictly economic factors; for instance, a part of the motivating force in the case of the banks seems to have been based on the fact that Government uses moral suasion from time to time in its dealings with the banks and that foreign controlled banks might be less responsive to such suasion than Canadian controlled firms.* It was a recognition of the need to use moral suasion that was partly at issue, not simply the economic importance of the banks.

In industry studies which will follow this Memorandum, a few additional key sectors will be examined to determine if some of the Government's non-economic objectives are being frustrated by non-Canadian control. In particular, the book publishing, magazine and film industries will be looked at from this viewpoint, as will parts of the natural resources and communications industries.** On the whole, however, it is not believed that there are a large number of additional sectors which ought to be designated as "key sectors" for reasons relating to non-economic objectives of the Government.

As for economic criteria for identifying key sectors, the main one used thus far seems to have been that based upon a concern to ensure Canadian control of the intermediation process, i.e. to make

---

* With respect to the other federally-incorporated financial institutions, it would appear that an important consideration has been a simple desire to maintain a Canadian presence in the industry.

** The relevant parts of the natural resource and communications industries are also looked at from economic perspectives.

sure financial intermediation is not in the hands of persons who are non-residents and who might siphon Canadian savings out of Canada to a greater degree than would residents.

On the other hand, it is possible to extend the definition of "key sectors" beyond that which has been used traditionally. As Cabinet directed specifically that criteria be proposed which would help permit decisions to be taken for the establishment of key sectors, this is done below.

Three kinds of criteria for the identification of key sectors are considered. They are described here as: "economic impact", and "non-economic". Each of these is considered in the sub-sections which follow below. However, it is important to recognize that these criteria are not ones which will determine in a clear cut and absolute fashion which sectors might be key sectors. Rather, they are criteria for helping to identify which sectors require detailed study as possible candidates for key sector status.

In a separate volume which will follow, such detailed studies are reported on in respect of the following industries: book publishing, magazine publishing, advertising, films, parts of natural resources (particularly mining and energy), parts of communications (computer utilities, data banks and telephones) most transportation sources and those parts of the financial industry in respect of which the Government does not now have a policy on the issue of ownership and control.

Economic Impact

The principle which would guide the Government in establishing key sectors for reasons of economic impact are the same as those which were discussed above in the section on the screening process. Basically, the view expressed there was that whenever the economic impact of foreign direct investment does not involve a transmission of net economic benefits to Canada, such investment ought to be blocked. Among the assumptions underlying this position is that whenever indigenous Canadian capabilities are equal to or better than foreign capabilities, or whenever industrial development considerations lead the Government to emphasize heavily a particular sector, this can constitute reason for insisting upon Canadian control.

The impact of foreign direct investment on the following factors would determine whether or not there was a net benefit being transmitted to Canada and thus whether a particular industry should be identified as a key sector

   a. the Government's industrial strategy (to the extent articulated);

b. productivity and industrial efficiency, including technological development;

c. the level of economic activity and employment;

d. the geographic location within Canada and the potential contribution of the investment to reducing regional disparities;

e. other economic benefits, (e.g. training and other spill-over benefits);

f. the extent to which the foreign entrant will stimulate competitive market forces in Canada, including the impact on prices and the quality of goods and services available in Canada.

That is, the guidelines discussed in the section on the screening agency are the same as those which help to determine the identification of key sectors. The same points are relevant. This also implies, however, that these sectors cannot be pre-determined. Careful case-by-case study is needed to determine if, for one reason or another, ownership of firms in a sector is a critical issue.

Such an approach is, by definition, a less absolutist approach to key sectors than has been undertaken in past policy. It involves the assumption that sectors can be key sectors for a period of years but that if a foreigner comes along with valuable new capacities or if the Canadian controlled firms become less efficient, a sector would cease enjoying this status.

Thus, the essence of this approach is that key sectors emerge out of one or another of two factors. The first is a comparison of indigenous Canadian and non-resident capacities in particular sectors of the economy through a period of time. Where Canadian capacities are equal or superior to those of non-residents, then rules could be developed involving a bias against foreign investment. These need not have the force of law but could serve simply as a guideline to a screening agency; alternatively, such a situation could be reflected in regulations pursuant to a general foreign investment law. In either case, it would always be open to the agency to agree to a foreign investment where the foreigner could demonstrate a uniqueness; or alternatively, if the protectionism inherent in ownership guidelines or regulations made the Canadian controlled firm less efficient, so that it was losing its comparative advantage, the guidelines or regulations could be modified to allow foreign controlled firms entry for the new competitive thrust they could provide. However, if a statute were in existence to deal with each key industry, more rigidity would be introduced. As the basis for such key sectors is rooted in an economic rationale, such rigidity seems not to be justified, as it would involve an economic cost.

The second is based on industrial strategy. When the economy, and possibly the Government, develops a large stake in an industry, it may wish to try to ensure Canadian control of that industry (e.g. STOL or telecommunication satellite). This is because Canadian control helps a firm to sink roots in Canada and such roots may be needed to ensure that the firm in question is not subject to arbitrary decisions by those who are not particularly responsive to Canadian market pressures or Canadian Government concerns (e.g. the R.C.A. case).

Both these factors — comparative advantage and industrial strategy — tend to influence some people to the view that natural resources should be designated a key sector.

Non-economic Factors: Cultural Activities

With respect to those industries which have an important role in the safeguarding and development of Canadian culture and identity, several considerations seem to be relevant. The first is that the total reliance upon foreign controlled firms in industries such as the production and distribution of magazines and books leaves open the possibility that these firms will serve as the vehicles through which foreign culture can come to dominate Canadian culture. If this were taken to an extreme, the consequences for indigenous cultural development and distinctive cultural identity would be very adverse. This does not mean that if foreign controlled firms do dominate, the worst would necessarily happen. Rather, it means that there is the ultimate risk of foreign cultural domination and that this risk is too great to take.

The converse situation is, of course, one where only Canadian controlled firms are allowed in cultural activities, and where all imports of foreign books, films, magazines, and works of art, etc. are prohibited, thus insulating Canada from the rest of the world's creative output. This extreme is equally reprehensible and obviously would never be the basis of Canadian cultural policy.

Between these extremes, there is room for much debate and argument about the appropriate role for the foreign controlled firm in Canada. These issues are examined in the volume which follows. At the same time, it must be recognized that any rationale, for either a restrictive or liberal ownership policy, is difficult to justify in the absence of a fairly full elaboration of the Government's cultural policy.

Conclusions

A foreign ownership policy based largely upon the concept of key sectors is one which is likely to be more economically costly than one based upon a screening process. In particular, it gives the Government less capacity to influence the domestic economic environment than does a screening process. This Memorandum therefore does not favour the use of this concept as the basis for Government policy.

At the same time, there may be some limited role for a key sector policy as a supplement to a screening process. If this is agreed upon, there are three groups of factors which can be useful in helping the Government to identify which sectors are key sectors. These factors are not absolutist, in the sense that they pre-determine which sectors will necessarily be designated as key sectors, but they do indicate those that merit special study to determine if they should be so designated.

In general, there do not appear to be many non-economic criteria which are important in helping to identify key sectors. However, such sectors as do seem to require study based upon non-economic considerations are considered in a separate volume. Similarly, specific industry studies have been undertaken in respect of those sectors which seem to have an economic impact which exceeds by a very substantial amount their own size in the economy, e.g. transportation, communications.

Finally, by applying the same criteria as are recommended to guide the screening process, it would be practicable to identify through time those sectors of the economy which should be reserved for Canadian control provided an administrative apparatus were in place for making the necessary decisions.

FIXED RULES AS AN APPROACH

Mandatory Canadian Shareholdings/Joint Venture

An alternative general approach to foreign ownership would be to legislate mandatory majority (51 per cent) or equal (50 per cent) Canadian shareholdings in all Canadian firms of economic significance. This proposal would be similar to that advanced by the Wahn Committee. Provisions of this kind are now also found in Mexican and Japanese legislation.

Even if foreign parents were given some time to gradually sell their shares, this proposal would assuredly result in a very substantial reduction in the degree of foreign ownership in Canadian busines enterprises. As such, it constitutes a clear alternative to the other general approaches (screening, exchange controls and key sectors) which were discussed above. Legislating minority Canadian share-holdings, or encouraging them, are also possible policy elements. However, steps of this kind, in themselves, are not really big enough to constitute an alternative general approach.

Like the key sector approach, but unlike the screening process, a policy based on fixed ownership rules assumes a certain real benefit is acquired in obtaining Canadian ownership per se or, at least, some degree of Canadian ownership. That is, the premises of the approach are very different than those in the screening process.

OPTIONS WITHIN THIS APPROACH

The idea of mandatory Canadian shareholdings could be developed in several ways. The spectrum of possibilities is illustrated by the examples below.

a. Joint ventures — one possibility is to require by law that all foreign investors in Canada be required to have a Canadian partner. The Canadian partner would have to hold at least 51 per cent (or 50 per cent) of the voting stock and would be entitled to elect directors in proportion to his share of voting stock, i.e. a joint venture. This would ensure both substantial Canadian equity participation and an important Canadian voice in the management of the company.

b. As a second option, the law could provide for 51 per cent (or more) Canadian ownership of voting stock, in *all* Canadian firms, or all firms of significant size, with directors to be elected separately by the Canadian and foreign shareholders. It would also be required that the directors be elected separately by Canadian and foreign shareholders in proportion to the size of their respective shareholdings. In that way, the directors chosen by Canadian shareholders would always be in the majority. The existing details of such a scheme could be altered but the concept here is clear. The law would provide both for Canadian ownership and, while not ensuring Canadian control, increase substantially the likelihood of this in that it would allow any group of Canadian shareholders who could obtain the support of half the Canadian share-holdings to be able to control the board of directors.

c. On the other hand, the above possibility (b) above), could be implemented, but without any requirement for separate election of Canadian directors. This would provide for substantial Canadian ownership. However, in most circumstances, the foreign affiliate would be able to retain effective control.

d. At the other end of the spectrum, the law could provide for minority Canadian shareholdings, say 25 or 33 per cent, with the aim primarily of providing Canadians with more opportunities to invest in Canada.

Finally, it is conceivable to achieve some of the above control objectives, (a) and (b) above, without requiring Canadians to provide for 50 or 51 per cent of the equity capital. For instance, common shares could be divided into several participating classes (class "A", class "B", class "C", etc.) but with only one class (say class "A") having voting rights. Thus, theoretically, it may be conceivable to effect Canadian control without requiring very large investments.

OPTION ONE – JOINT VENTURES

Under this possibility, legislation would be passed requiring that all foreign direct investment in Canada be made with a Canadian partner who would hold either 50 or 51 per cent of the voting shares and who would be entitled to elect a corresponding proportion of directors. In this approach, all of the shares held by Canadian citizens would be concentrated in one Canadian firm, so that the foreign shareholding would not be the largest single concentration of shares (as would be the case if the law provided only for 50 or 51 per cent Canadian ownership but with the possibility of the Canadian shareholdings being fragmented).

Apart from the symbolic act of reducing foreign control, little of economic value would be achieved. The costs would be great, needed investment would be lost and truncation would increase. There might be greater inefficiency in Canadian management. Thus, such a policy across all industries is unrealistic.

OPTION TWO – LEGISLATING MAJORITY CANADIAN OWNERSHIP WITH A MAJORITY ON THE BOARD OF DIRECTORS TO REPRESENT THEM

In the second option postulated above, all firms of economic significance would have 51 per cent or more Canadian ownership of voting stock. Canadian shareholders and foreign shareholders would each elect a separate slate of shareholders. If 51 per cent of the shares were owned by Canada, 51 per cent of the directors would be chosen by the Canadian shareholders. Any group of Canadian shareholders which could muster the support of half of the Canadian shareholders (i.e. 25.6 per cent of the total voting shares) could elect its slate of directors. This would make it possible to obtain control.

It would, of course, also be possible for the foreign affiliate to persuade a Canadian shareholder to nominate a slate of Canadian directors that were sympathetic to the foreigner's position. The foreign affiliate would have the resources to mount a campaign to have elected candidates it preferred to represent Canadian shareholders. At the same time, it would always be possible for a Canadian group, which wished to build the subsidiary into a company, relatively independent of the foreign affiliate, or which wished to increase the profits of the subsidiary at the expense of the parent, to gain control. The foreign investor would be conscious of this. He would recognize that his hold on the Canadian firm was not a sure one.

This approach is thus similar to the joint venture in that it involves 51 (or 50) per cent Canadian ownership. It differs in that it does not ensure that the Canadian ownership will be concentrated, even though it does leave open this possibility.

In assessing the implications of this approach for the various issues which are of concern in this Memorandum, little different need be said than was indicated above in the assessment of mandatory joint ventures. The foreign investor will recognize that he would be entitled to only 49 per cent of the profits. He would recognize that his capacity to benefit in other ways would be threatened by the possibility of Canadian control.

Thus, the incentive to truncate would be such as described above. The likelihood of reduced foreign investment would be as great, thus increasing protectionism and jeopardizing economic efficiency. The lack of selectivity would similarly involve a large economic cost. None of the costs would change greatly. The arguments, in short, would be equally against such an approach.

OPTION THREE – LEGISLATING 51 PER CENT CANADIAN OWNERSHIP

The third option set out at the beginning was for the Government to legislate 51 per cent Canadian ownership but without any provision for separate election of Canadian directors by Canadian shareholders. In most cases, this would involve continued foreign control.

In summary, there are no striking arguments in favour of this approach, other than the purely symbolic gesture of having 51 per cent of all firms owned by Canadians. On the other hand, there are very striking arguments against it, particularly the likelihood of substantial greater truncation and, secondly, the likelihood that further Canadian control of Canadian business would be endangered by the fragmentation of Canadian capital.

OPTION FOUR – MINORITY CANADIAN SHAREHOLDERS

Under this last option, Canadian law would provide that all foreign controlled firms must have at least 25 or 33 per cent Canadian ownership of voting shares.

Two objectives might be served by such a law. Firstly, increased opportunities would be made available to Canadians to invest in Canadian firms. Secondly, greater Canadian ownership might in turn lead to election of more Canadian directors with the possibility that the subsidiaries would be sensitized to the needs of Canada and thus more responsive to the Canadian environment and public policy.

The same objections that were cited above in respect of 51 per cent Canadian ownership option (option three) would apply also here. Incentive to truncate would remain quite striking – though not quite as striking as in the case immediately above – and difficult concerning Canadian firms in raising equity capital might increase. However, they would obviously not increase as much as if the situation were 50 per cent equity offered to Canadians.

PROBLEMS IN ESTABLISHING THE SELLING PRICE IF MANDATORY OWNERSHIP RULES ARE IMPLEMENTED

As a practical matter, if a law were passed requiring foreign controlled firms to make shares available to Canadians, it would be necessary to allow for a fairly long period of time over which this requirement could be implemented. If this were not done, the result would be a flood of shares on the Canadian market, which inevitably would far exceed the demand for such shares. The result would be that the price per share would likely be substantially lower than a realistic market value. In turn, this would likely lead to strenuous opposition from the foreign controlled firms, with the support of their home governments. Either the Canadian Government would then have to step in and establish appropriate values – never an easy business – or a major row would result with our major trading partners.

A further consideration is that a Canadian investor's view of the value of the shares of a Canadian subsidiary is likely to be different from that of the parent firm. It was suggested earlier that the subsidiary, especially in manufacturing, is often very heavily dependent upon the parent's technology, know-how and marketing channels. It is linked closely to the parent's strategy and capable of contributing to it. In cases where the subsidiaries are forced to an arms length relationship with the parent, as would be the case in the first two of the options discussed in this section, Canadian investors might anticipate some reduction in profits, as the parent firms would be more insistent upon full value for goods and services it provided.

Thus the implementation would have to be spread over a good number of years — to allow the market to set the value fairly.

General Conclusions on Mandatory Canadian Shareholding

The weight of evidence and argument is strongly against any approach based upon mandatory shareholdings. Apart from this symbolic gesture such benefits as might be obtained would be very small. The economic costs involved would vary from one option to the other. But in all cases they would be substantial. Accordingly, this Memorandum does not recommend in favour of such an approach.

OPTIONAL CANADIAN SHAREHOLDING

There is one additional possibility that can be considered, in the event that it is decided to implement the recommended screening process. This is to make it known that the Government generally considers that it is desirable for foreign controlled firms to allow Canadians some substantial degree of equity participation in subsidiaries.

Some of the arguments outlined above with respect to mandatory Canadian shareholdings would apply also in this case, especially the concern that this would increase the likelihood of truncation. Against this argument must be set the possibility that such firms would appoint external Canadian directors — indeed if some priority is given to having Canadian shareholdings then equal priority should be given to requiring external Canadian directors. This could result in greater sensitivity to the Canadian environment and indirectly be of some assistance in that respect.

On balance, it is proposed that if the screening agency is established, the willingness to make shares available to Canadians should be viewed as one consideration, but not a major one, in evaluating foreign direct investment.

CANADIAN DIRECTORS

The aim of this section is to consider whether the Government should develop special rules to encourage or require foreign controlled firms to appoint Canadian citizens who are ordinarily resident in Canada to their boards of directors. In considering some of the possible policy alternatives outlined below, a number of factors must be taken into account.

Firstly, a major consideration is whether having Canadians on the board of directors of a subsidiary would enable the interests of the subsidiary to be asserted more forcefully within the multinational enterprise than it would be without them. The interests of the subsidiary do at times differ from the parent's. On occasion, the subsidiary will want to be able to talk fairly toughly to the parent in presenting a viewpoint. In view of this, the existence of external Canadian directors (external directors refers to directors who are not officers of the subsidiary or otherwise linked to it in a business relationship, e.g., its fiscal agent or legal counsel) could be of some importance in such situations, especially as boards of directors of subsidiaries are not now normally very strong bodies. Where Canadian minority shareholders also exist, an even greater weight would likely be given to the views of Canadian directors by the parent firm. On the whole, however, the capacity of any board of directors of a subsidiary to convince a parent is not very great where there is a real difference of interest. Thus the benefits involved are likely to be modest.

A second consideration relates to the role of directors under company law. The Department of Consumer and Corporate Affairs is now beginning to consider further revisions to the Canada Corporations Act which would make directors more directly responsible for the affairs of a company and consequently oblige them to take a greater interest and participate more actively in its activities. This could tend also to enhance the value of having Canadian directors.

In summary, some measures in this field would be helpful but it must be recognized that their beneficial impact is bound to be modest.

APPOINTING GOVERNMENT NOMINEES TO BOARDS OF DIRECTORS OF LARGE MULTINATIONAL FIRMS

It would not be illogical that the Government be given the authority to appoint directors to large MNEs — possibly the Federal Government appointing one and the Provincial Government most concerned, a second.

The function of Government appointed members of a board of directors could be the same as that of any other Canadian director, except that this would give much greater assurance that the director in question was not simply a 'dummy' appointee of the parent company, but was really free to argue for and defend the interests of the Canadian corporation. In other words, the purpose of such an appointment would not be to secure a director who would report back to the Government on the corporation's affairs, but to assure an active and independent Canadian voice in the affairs of these companies.

To ensure that this was most effective, it would be desirable that such directors be assured a public platform for their views. If there were Canadian shareholders, and hence an annual public meeting, this meeting could provide the necessary platform. If there were no public annual meeting, an alternative platform would have to be developed. In other words, where the director felt that the interests of the Canadian subsidiary were not being fully protected, he would be free to present his view publicly. Short of this, the only course open to a Government appointed director would be resignation.

The implementation of such a proposal would be a recognition of two factors: firstly, that the Canadian subsidiaries can and sometimes do have interests which differ from those of the parents; and secondly, the important role of subsidiaries in the Canadian economy. At the same time, there is no hiding that such a proposal would be considered a very radical innovation and opposed strongly by the business community.

As such a radical step is most required only in respect of the largest and most powerful MNEs, such measures could be restricted to the largest firms — say those with assets of $50 million. This would apply to all multinational firms, whether they were Canadian or foreign owned, thus easing to some degree accusations of discrimination.

As a way of improving the net benefits to Canada from foreign direct investment, this technique would obviously be much less effective than a screening process, and most effective as a supplement to it. Its novelty, however, and the fact that the international business community is not accustomed to this form of intervention (unlike a screening process) may make this step impractical politically at this time.

MANDATORY CANADIAN DIRECTORSHIPS IN FOREIGN CONTROLLED FIRMS

A number of countries do attach some importance to having

their nationals appointed to the boards of directors of foreign controlled firms in their jurisdiction (e.g., Australia, Norway). The feeling generally seems to be that this helps the foreign controlled firm to understand the economic, political and social environment of the host country and appreciate better its cultural distinctions. It may also be intended to help integrate the foreign controlled firms into the host environment and to help them contribute more effectively to the local economy.

The question thus arises as to whether all foreign controlled firms ought to be required to appoint to their boards of directors a minimum proportion of Canadian citizens ordinarily resident in Canada (say one-half). If the proposed screening process is implemented, this could be done by the law directing the screening agency to reject proposals for investments in Canada where this provision was not complied with. Other ways of achieving this objective also exist (e.g. providing a law that all foreign controlled firms incorporate federally and requiring as a condition of such incorporation that a designated proportion of the directors be Canadian citizens resident in Canada).

An alternative to this possible policy element is for the Government to direct the screening agency, if implemented, to take account of a willingness to appoint Canadian citizens as directors in evaluating a foreign investment. The appointment of Canadian directors would then not be a mandatory requirement but simply one factor to be taken into account. If that is done, it is proposed that the willingness to appoint Canadian directors, like the willingness to allow for minority Canadian shareholdings, should not be a major consideration in the eyes of a screening agency.

The appointment of Canadian directors in itself is not a step of great significance. The Canadian director can simply be the figure-head for the parent company's management; or he can be someone of independent strength and standing. However, it is hard to conceive of firms, which are not interested in having Canadian directors, selecting the latter type of person.

No great improvements in the performance of foreign controlled firms are likely to result from making Canadian directorships mandatory. In conjunction with other proposals in this Memorandum it could add some small measure of improved performance and it is proposed that such a measure be considered in the context of the review of the Canada Corporations Act.

APPOINTMENT OF SEPARATE CANADIAN DIRECTORS TO BE ELECTED BY CANADIAN MINORITY SHAREHOLDERS INTERESTS

It has been suggested in the previous sub-section that Canadian public policy should contain only a small bias in favour of Canadian minority shareholdings in foreign controlled firms. If any such bias is present, it is important that the interests of Canadian shareholders should be adequately protected.

It will be apparent that there are times when the interests of the Canadian subsidiary may differ from the global interests of the MNE. At such times, on the assumption that there are no Canadian shareholders, it is easy for the MNE to put its overall interests first.

If there are Canadian shareholders, however, it will be important to make sure that the foreign parent does not take undue advantage of that situation. Indeed, if there are minority Canadian shareholders, due to the policy of the Federal Government, it is even more fully the responsibility of the Federal Government to provide adequate protection for the Canadian shareholder.

One way to help give this needed protection is by providing that Canadian shareholders may elect separately Canadian directors. In the event that the interests of the Canadian shareholders were not protected, these directors could be dismissed.

While this Memorandum does not argue strongly in favour of the desirability of minority Canadian shareholders, it is proposed that if Ministers do decide to attach some priority to this concept, they should be prepared to support the Canadian shareholders. This could be done by giving them protection, probably along the lines set out here, by including the needed proposals in amendments to the Canadian Corporations Act.

Conclusions

The important role of subsidiaries in the Canadian economy and the scope for difference of interest between the parent and its subsidiary both lead logically to the need for Government appointees to the larger and more important of MNE corporations. Political difficulties however, are likely to make this impractical at this time.

On the other hand, the Government could empower the screening agency, if that proposal is implemented, to take account of the proportion of external directors who are Canadian citizens ordinarily resident in Canada. Alternatively the Government could require all foreign controlled firms to appoint a minimum proportion of Canadian citizens ordinarily resident in Canada as external directors. In the event that revisions to the Canada Corporations Act are implemented in a way which would oblige directors to take greater responsibility for corporate affairs, this might have some modest favourable impact upon the Canadian economy.

Finally, if the Government does choose to promote strongly the desirability of foreign subsidiaries making available equity to minority Canadian shareholders, the issue arises as to whether the Government does not also have an obligation to ensure that their interests are sufficiently protected. One way of doing this would be by allowing Canadian minority shareholders to elect directors separately from foreign shareholders.

8

OTHER GOVERNMENT POLICIES

POSSIBLE FURTHER MEASURES TO INCREASE CANADIAN CONTROL OF CANADIAN BUSINESS

Rationale for Increasing Canadian Ownership

In this section, proposals are considered as a technique for increasing Canadian control. They are:

a. discriminating in Government purchases of goods and services in favour of Canadian controlled firms;

b. discriminating in Government grant and loan programmes in favour of Canadian controlled firms;

c. discriminating through the tax system in favour of Canadian controlled firms.

Each of these policy instruments is examined further below.

Government and Crown Corporation Procurement

INTRODUCTION

It has been estimated that approximately $4 billion is spent annually for the procurement of goods and services by federal, provincial and municipal governments exclusive of property, construction and building materials. Of this amount, almost half is purchased by the Department of Supply and Services and other Federal Government departments and agencies, including Crown Corporations. Being such a large purchaser, it is possible, in theory at least, for the Federal Government to have a significant impact on the pattern and extent of foreign control of Canadian business enterprise. At the extreme, it could prohibit all purchases of goods and services from foreign controlled firms. The issue which must be considered is how far down such a path it would be reasonable to go in order to increase Canadian ownership.

THE AIMS OF PROCUREMENT POLICY

The primary function of a procurement policy should be to obtain the best value for money spent. This involves identifying reliable sources, securing the lowest possible price subject to reasonable assurances in respect of quality, delivery, service, etc. and performing these functions with the lowest feasible administration cost.

PREFERENCE FOR CANADIAN FIRMS

Notwithstanding the arguments in favour of a best value for dollar spent approach to procurement, the present Government purchasing system in fact contains deviations from this method, due to other Government objectives. For instance, because of a Government concern about the level of employment, preference for Canadian content may be affected through sourcing procedures, which apply both to Crown Corporations and Government Departments. These procedures are usually established on the basis of administrative rulings, by Treasury Board in some cases, but more usually by the operating department of Crown Corporations. Normally, an effort is made to obtain a sufficient number of bids to establish "competition", but an upper limit on the number of bids may also be set to reduce time required to evaluate them. As a generalization, in cases where goods are easily specified and available from a number of sources, buying agencies will purchase by soliciting all those firms who have expressed an interest in bidding on the particular item required. The other end of the "sourcing" spectrum is the case where there is only one supplier who can meet the specification for the merchandise in the required time frame. In buying custom-built equipment or equipment having a high engineering content or high technical risk, it is common practice to solicit bids selectively from 5 or 6 firms based on an analysis of the equipment required and of the individual firm's qualifications in terms of management, engineering, production, quality control, service, etc.

In addition to sourcing in Canada wherever practicable, Departments are under Cabinet directive to use Canadian labour and materials wherever possible subject to the qualification to the effect that no more than a 10 per cent premium should be paid for Canadian content. The Canadian labour and materials clause is in the standard form for Government construction contracts or something like it appears in most of the purchase contract forms used by Departments.

The prohibition is only against exceeding a 10 per cent premium without Treasury Board approval. It is not explicitly an order to pay the premium wherever it is possible to make a purchase of Canadian content by paying the premium.

In cases where foreign bids have been allowed by Departments, despite the allowance and any tariffs applying to imported goods, Canadians have often not been successful in obtaining the contract.

In general, there have been very few explicit conditions placed on Crown Corporations to bias their procurement policy toward Canadian suppliers. The 10 per cent clause has had even less effect on the Corporations than on the Departments, because of their greater degree of independence.

SHOULD PROCUREMENT POLICY DISCRIMINATE IN FAVOUR OF CANADIAN CONTROLLED FIRMS?

While past preferences in procurement have been aimed at Canadian content, not country of control, it would be technically feasible to build a preference for Canadian controlled firms into Government procurement policies so long as a clear cut definition of control were provided.

While preference could be given in favour of Canadian controlled firms the question would still remain as to whether this would be an effective instrument for increasing the degree of Canadian control in the economy. If the preference were absolute (i.e. if foreign controlled firms were not permitted to bid) discrimination would be effective if the industry were at all reliant upon Government contracts. But in many instances the price would be enormous. To take an extreme illustration, if the Government were to insist today that all future purchases of aircraft by the Armed Forces and Air Canada be from firms which are Canadian controlled, this would in turn necessitate the establishment of a Canadian controlled capital intensive, technically advanced industry, of a kind which is not now in Canada. For a good number of years, this would be bound in effect to involve hundreds of millions of dollars of annual subsidies to meet the Canadian ownership and control objective.

Such discrimination would open up the possibility of the Government paying higher prices for goods and services in a much wider range of cases than it now does. Moreover, with such a general rule, it would be very difficult to predict the total annual cost to the Treasury, though it is more likely to be in the tens of millions rather than hundreds of millions.

CONCLUSIONS

There is some precedent for Crown Corporations and Departments using procurement to achieve goals of national policy other than those directly related to the objectives of the buying agency.

Secondly, the constraint represented by the necessity of meeting user requirements within some reasonable financial limits reduces the potential effectiveness of the procurement tool for reducing the degree of foreign control. It would also be necessary to consider reimbursing user departments and/or corporation budgets to the extent that preferences are applied. Such reimbursement would most likely be required in the case of Crown Corporations. Current "responsibility accounting" policies now being introduced into management of Departments also strengthens the argument for such compensation in this area as well.

Thirdly, a generalized procurement preference for Canadian controlled firms is feasible. However, such a shotgun approach could be costly in relation to the return likely to be obtained from it in terms of increased Canadian ownership.

However, a more selective approach is practical. There are sectors of the Canadian economy which are influenced significantly by Federal Government procurement. The sectors where Government procurement is large and might conceivably provide a lever, are shipbuilding and repair, aircraft and parts, communications equipment (including avionics), railroad rolling stock and scientific and professional equipment. These sectors are largely foreign controlled at the moment but over time, selective procurement could strengthen Canadian capacities in at least some of the sub-sectors involved.

Grant and Loan Programme

INTRODUCTION

The objectives of this sub-section are to: show how Canadian Government grants, loans and insured loans are awarded as between Canadian and non-resident controlled firms; consider the possibility of restricting the grants, loans and insured loans to Canadian controlled firms as a technique of increasing Canadian control in the economy; consider whether such grants and loans can be used as a lever for insisting on performance undertakings by foreign controlled firms, where the grants and loans are not already oriented toward specific performance requirements.

It is concluded that foreign controlled firms benefit substantially from some of the programmes, particularly those oriented to specific

Government objectives rather than those aimed simply at the providing of Government financial assistance to industry. It is also concluded that cases where such specific Government objectives exist (such as regional expansion, industrial research and innovation) it would not be practicable to restrict grants to Canadian controlled firms as this would clearly reduce the benefit to cost ratio of these programmes and these other Government objectives would suffer.

Where the funds are less closely tied to fairly narrow and detailed Government objectives (e.g., IDB, GAAP) it would be possible to discriminate in favour of Canadian controlled firms without jeopardizing the achievement of the policy objectives involved. This Memorandum recommends in favour of such a course. It also recommends that in the event that Cabinet decides against screening foreign takeovers, Canadian controlled firms receiving such GAAP and IDB assistance grants should, as a condition of receiving the assistance, be obliged to adopt constrained share status whereby they would undertake in their letters patent that 75 per cent or more of the outstanding shares of the company would always remain in Canadian hands, unless the Government allowed for foreign acquisition.

As for the performance undertakings from foreign controlled firms in return for grants and loans, such undertakings actually exist up to a point in cases where the grants or loans are performance or project oriented. In other cases, this issue would not arise if Cabinet were to accept the proposal that these other programmes be restricted to Canadian controlled firms.

THE ADEQUACY OF INFORMATION

Introduction

Vast amounts of statistical and other types of information on Canadian corporations, both resident and foreign controlled, are collected by various Government departments and agencies. This information covers practically all aspects of company financial and other operations — statements of income and expenditure, source and uses of funds, surplus, balance sheet information, investment and investment intentions, ownership, production, employment, international trade, sales, profits, R&D, wages and salaries, value added, and management (directors and senior officers).

Qualitative or non-statistical information useful for policy purposes (e.g. about marketing policies, licensing arrangements, R&D policies, the organization, structure, and functioning of companies) is collected by the D.B.S., Departments of Finance, Industry, Trade & Commerce, Energy, Mines & Resources, and Consumer & Corporat Affairs, in connection with various departmental programmes, e.g., trade and industrial development, combines administration, etc.

Although this plethora of information is collected by departments and agencies of the Federal Government, most of it may be available to the public and/or Government policy makers in aggregate form only, e.g., the Statistics Act, the Income Tax Act, and to some extent, the Corporations and Labour Unions Returns Act preclude the divulgence of individual company information for purposes other than those for which it was collected.

The adequacy of information available on the corporate sector can only be judged in relation to the purposes of the potential users. Because the number of potential users and the purposes to be served are so numerous and so diverse, no general answer to the question of adequacy can be given: what is adequate for the Ph.D. student writing a dissertation may not be adequate for his professor on contract to a Government department; what is adequate for the investment analyst may not be adequate for the Government policy maker; what is adequate (in aggregate terms) for the Bank of Canada may not be adequate (in sectoral terms) for the Department of Industry, Trade & Commerce.

The Identification of Foreign Owned and Controlled Companies

Important to all four purposes indicated above is the identification of which companies are foreign controlled and the changes in the degree of foreign control over time. This information is the fundamental building block without which it would be impossible to have a policy on foreign control of the domestic economic environment.

Control of a corporation is normally exercised through the ownership of over 50 per cent of its voting stock. However, control can be exercised in other ways:

    a. by a minority holding of voting rights if the ownership of the voting stock is widely diffused;

    b. by the ownership of corporate debt;

    c. by purchase or supply contracts;

    d. through licensing arrangements and franchises;

    e. through management contracts or informal understandings with management;

    f. through voting trusts, shareholder agreements, or other contractual arrangements, including potential control through securities, pledged agreements, or trust indenture that arises in case of default.

Both CALURA and the International Investment Position (IIP) compiled in the Balance of Payments Section (BOP) of the D.B.S. collect information on the ownership of voting stock. This information is also collected for the Guidelines programme of the Department of Industry, Trade & Commerce for a limited number of companies. However, the concept of control used in these three cases is slightly different. In the CALURA series, a company is considered to be foreign controlled if 50 per cent or more of its voting stock is known to be held outside Canada, or by one or more Canadian companies which are, in turn, foreign controlled. IIP statistics record an enterprise as foreign controlled if 50 per cent or more of its voting stock is held *in one country* outside Canada. The enterprise includes all the corporations over which the foreign parent company or group of shareholders are in a position to exercise control. For the Industry, Trade & Commerce Guidelines programme a Canadian company is regarded as foreign controlled if 50 per cent of its voting stock is owned by one foreign parent.

Conclusions

There is an important difference between the Government requesting information from a corporation and from a private individual. A corporation is an aggregation of power with perpetual life and, in most cases, limited liability. It is also a creature of the state enjoying certain rights and having certain obligations in law. It is to be expected that its creator should wish to keep informed about its activities, particularly when the decisions of the corporations have a widespread public impact. Firms which help to determine the salary and work conditions of ten or twenty thousand people, which play a leading role in our trade, which are causing or combatting environmental problems are simply not individuals. Thus, what might be regarded as "snooping" in relation to an individual, should not be so regarded in relation to a corporation.

Vast amounts of statistical and other information on Canadian corporations, both Canadian and foreign controlled, are collected by various Government departments and agencies but some significant gaps exist either because the data are not collected, or they are collected and not published. Government policy makers do not have access to much of the data collected by the Dominion Bureau of Statistics because of the secrecy provisions of the Statistics Act.

There are four broad purposes for which corporate information may be required in relation to domestic control of the national economic environment:

a. the identification of foreign controlled companies;
b. economic analysis of the costs and benefits of foreign ownership in the Canadian economy in aggregate terms;
c. the implementation of a screening process for direct foreign investment;
d. the possible increase in Canadian control of business activity through improved disclosure (e.g., profits by product line). This could lead to the retention of more savings in Canada ar to the attraction of more Canadians into the market place to exploit profit opportunities identified by better disclosure, especially on the part of foreign controlled companies.

Recommendations

Some of the recommendations involve considerable changes in the existing system of collecting and aggregating data and could on be implemented as part of a phased programme.

IDENTIFICATION OF CONTROL

1. The statistical definition of control should be standardized using the definition developed by the D.B.S. for IIP statistics Ownership statistics should continue to be published using both ownership concepts as each is useful for different purposes.

2. More resources should be devoted to the problem of identify ing effective control of Canadian companies which may man fest itself in other ways than majority ownership of a company's voting stock. The responsibility for this should re with the Minister to whom the screening authorities report. The D.B.S. should be informed of these decisions in order to consider whether changes are required in their statistical series. The screening agency should maintain a register of foreign controlled companies and the public should have access to this information. A list of changes in control could be published monthly in the Canada Gazette.

3. Legislative authority should exist in either the D.B.S. or the screening agency or both to require banks, trust companies c other nominees to divulge the owners of nominee accounts i required for the purpose of identifying foreign control.

ECONOMIC ANALYSIS

4. Rather than operating three major statistical programmes which relate (at least in part) to foreign controlled companies, the Government should concentrate on the improvement of one of these. The IT&C Guidelines programme should be abolished and Section B of Part I of the CALURA Act repealed. Making use of the general statistical power, the D.B.S. should publish an annual review of foreign ownership and control in the Canadian economy, with a greater number of statistical series breaking out the Canadian controlled and the foreign controlled sectors.

5. Consideration should be given to concentrating resources in a single group within the D.B.S. with its own priorities related to foreign direct investment.

6. The data for economic analysis should be improved by: (a) the subdivision of basic statistical series between Canadian controlled and foreign controlled firms and by country of origin; (b) filling the gaps in information — particularly the data on international transactions (foreign trade by individual companies, non-merchandise transactions, etc.), sources of funds, retained earnings in Canada, etc. Where relevant these data should show the country of source or destination and indicate whether the transaction was between affiliates; (c) the publication of industrial statistics relating to foreign ownership using the Standard Industrial Classification.

7. D.B.S. reports dealing with foreign ownership and control should concentrate on control rather than ownership but statistical series in CALURA and the IIP dealing with ownership should be continued.

8. The D.B.S., in cooperation with interested departments and agencies should determine which statistical series should be published annually, which regularly but not annually, and which only occasionally.

9. If the compilation of data on foreign control involves the use of a size criterion as at present under CALURA, the D.B.S. should undertake periodic surveys of corporations excluded by this criterion.

10. In seeking to determine intercorporate links, information on the ownership of shares should be requested not only from corporations (as at present under CALURA) but also from *persons*.

11. The OECD could be asked to consider coordinating, introducing, and maintaining a series of statistics on the behaviour of foreign controlled companies in various countries.

SCREENING PROCESS

12. The screening agency should have legislative authority to obtain information required for the operation of the screening mechanism. It will also need basic economic and industrial information on individual companies similar to that received by the IT&C Guidelines programme and by the D.B.S. If the agency cannot obtain this material from the D.B.S., then it should have legislative authority to obtain it direct from Canadian companies whether Canadian or foreign controlled. The agency will also need legislative authority to require companies to report on the fulfilment of any undertakings given to the screening authorities. The screening authorities should have, through legislation, general investigative power and the authority to scrutinize particular commercial transactions. There should be penalties for noncompliance.

13. Changes in the reporting requirement to the screening authorities should be able to be made through Order-in-Council (i.e., not require legislation as at present under CALURA).

14. The screening agency should undertake special studies on foreign ownership as directed by the responsible Minister.

15. The screening agency should have access to the information collected on foreign controlled companies by other Governmental departments and agencies such as the C.R.T.C., the C.T.C., the Department of Insurance, etc., to the extent necessary to ensure that the broad objectives of the Government's foreign ownership policy are being met in these fields.

16. The screening agency should keep a record of all Governmental assistance to foreign controlled firms whether originating from the Federal or Provincial Government.

DISCLOSURE

The revised Canada Corporations Act does not take us very far towards disclosure of the operations of individual companies, especially those that are private and foreign controlled. The disclosure requirements of the Canada Corporations Act should be improved to bring them more in line with those required by the SEC in the U.S. When the Department of Consumer & Corporate Affairs undertakes further amendment of the Canada Corporations Act now under preparation, it should consider the feasibility of requiring all foreign controlled companies to be federally incorporated.

CANADIAN MULTINATIONAL COMPANIES

The competitive ability and market power of multinational corporations suggest that it would be to Canada's advantage to foster the development of Canadian multinational companies at least in some of those sectors where internationalization is occurring and where Canada has a comparative advantage. The alternatives would be to have branch plants of foreign multinationals operating in Canada, or to shut out multinationals altogether, thereby denying Canada the efficiencies which multinational corporations, in some cases, can generate, e.g., lower costs, increased competition, etc.

There are other advantages which would flow from having Canadian multinational companies with headquarters in Canada:

a. strategic corporate decisions and the "brains" of the corporation would be located in Canada. This would provide more challenging employment for Canadian managers, scientists, and other professionals. More importantly, the location of this "techno-structure" within Canada would also help to create a more stimulating entrepreneurial environment and help to counter the "branch plant mentality" which appears to be all too common at present;

b. with the headquarters and the strategic decision making functions located in Canada, it is more likely that vital activities such as R&D would take place in Canada. There would be a reduced tendency to truncate the Canadian operation. The likelihood of product and technological development tailored to Canadian needs could increase rather than Canadian tastes having to adjust to products and technologies developed abroad. With important assets in Canada, the Canadian Government would have greater influence over the operations of such firms;

c. while available evidence indicates that it is some time before the balance of payments effects from foreign direct investment are positive, Canada would benefit from the inflow of dividends, interest payments, management, R&D and other service payments from subsidiaries to the parent company. Against any positive balance of payments effects would have to be weighed any location of economic activity abroad which otherwise might have been located in Canada;.

d. the existence of a number of strong Canadian multinational companies would give Canada a place at the bargaining table in any international discussions relating to the MNE;

e. the existence of a number of strong Canadian multinational companies would serve to increase Canada's international prestige.

Problems for Canada in Encouraging Canadian MNEs

There are, at present, a number of Canadian controlled multi-national companies headquartered in Canada, e.g., the banks, Alcan, Polymer, Massey Ferguson, MacMillan Bloedel, Moore Corporation, Seagrams and Crush International. According to the D.B.S., Canadian direct investment abroad in 1964 totalled $3.5 billion. Non-residents controlled 47 per cent of these investments, (e.g., Ford's subsidiary in South Africa). The 13 largest firms accounted for 70 per cent of the total.

From the point of view of Canadian interests, experience to date with Canadian multinationals has not been entirely satisfactory. There appears to be a tendency for Canadian companies that become more international during their maturation to become less Canadian to the point where, in some instances, their Canadian identity becomes nominal, e.g., Inco and Massey Ferguson. Trying to draw up a list of important Canadian controlled MNEs underscores the problem. For example, are Alcan and Seagrams really Canadian controlled? The large and powerful U.S. market is a constant attraction for Canadian direct investment. Even Polymer, a Government owned corporation, has considered establishing a major expansion of its Sarnia operations in the U.S. Polymer has pointed to the need for a major facility within the large U.S. market, (i.e., to be "in" the market), the possibility of supplying materials under U.S. aid programmes, and the insurance against possible U.S. governmental actions which could affect North American marketing operations.

Policy Towards Canadian MNEs

Ensuring that the benefits of Canadian multinational corporations remain in Canada could be achieved through a number of policies. Canada could foster and encourage the development of multinationals in those sectors where ties to Canada are likely to be sufficiently strong to counteract the tendency to move out of Canada at the stage of maturity, e.g., some resource sectors and technologies specifically related to Canadian geographical or other needs. This however, is likely to be a difficult task. Even in the resource industries, where the ore body or cheap power should tie the operation to Canada, there seems to be a tendency for companies to gravitate from Canada, e.g., Inco and Alcan. Transfer pricing problems could be taken care of by more assiduous administration of Canadian laws on the subject. The Government could use R&D grants, other forms of Governmental assistance, and procurement policies and practices to ensure that certain activities remain in

Canada. The C.D.C. could also be used as an instrument to help keep a Canadian multinational "Canadian" by purchasing a proportion of equity and having a representative on the Board of Directors. Alternatively, the Government itself might buy 5 or 10 per cent of some Canadian MNEs in order to keep their roots in Canada. Other western governments have, for various reasons, found it to be in the national interest to invest in some of their large domestic firms.

Ministers should note that a policy to encourage the development of Canadian MNEs, at least in certain sectors, will affect the scope of any international initiatives the Government may wish to take to control the growth and power of MNEs in general. It would be difficult for the Government to launch an international initiative to control the powers of the MNE and at the same time implement policies to develop Canadian MNEs.

Conclusion

The general position on MNEs suggested in this Memorandum is that they should be encouraged where they are required to obtain better performance and that they should be discouraged where an international structure is not necessary for superior performance. The Government's policy towards Canadian MNEs should be basically similar, i.e., Canada should have a carefully thought out policy of encouraging development of Canadian multinational companies in some of the sectors that are multinational in character and where Canada has an actual or potential comparative advantage. In most cases, it is probably better to have the headquarters than the branch plant of the multinational enterprise in Canada. The alternative would be to shut out MNEs altogether but this would deny Canada the benefits in R&D, production, marketing, and promotion which these multinationals can bring in some sectors.